# Suburban Strains

# A Musical Play

## Book and lyrics
Alan Ayckbourn

## Music
Paul Todd

*Samuel French – London*
*New York – Sydney – Toronto – Hollywood*

Please note our NEW ADDRESS:

Samuel French Ltd
52 Fitzroy Street London W1P 6JR
Tel: 01 - 387 9373

# SUBURBAN STRAINS

First presented at the Stephen Joseph Theatre in the Round, Scarborough, on 18th January 1980 with the following cast of characters:

| | |
|---|---|
| **Caroline,** a teacher | Lavinia Bertram |
| **Kevin,** her husband | Robin Bowerman |
| **Douglas,** her father | John Arthur |
| **Jilly,** a film director | Alison Skilbeck |
| **Ivor,** her husband | Jeffrey Robert |
| **Matthew,** a doctor | Robin Herford |
| **Anne,** his wife | Alison Skilbeck |
| **Howard,** a gourmet | John Arthur |
| **Joanna,** an actress | Nina Edwards |
| **Miss Dent,** a teacher | Alison Skilbeck |
| **Linda,** a schoolgirl | Nina Edwards |
| **Naylor,** an industrialist | John Arthur |
| **Mr Grubland,** an OAP | Jeffrey Robert |
| **2nd OAP** | Robin Herford |
| **3rd OAP** | Alison Skilbeck |

Subsequently presented at the Round House, London, on 5th February, 1981, with the following cast of characters:

| | |
|---|---|
| **Caroline** | Lavinia Bertram |
| **Kevin** | Michael Simkins |
| **Douglas** | Russell Dixon |
| **Jilly** | Marcia Warren |
| **Ivor** | Graeme Eton |
| **Matthew** | Robin Herford |
| **Anne** | Marcia Warren |
| **Howard** | Russell Dixon |
| **Joanna** | Tessa Peake-Jones |
| **Miss Dent** | Marcia Warren |
| **Linda** | Tessa Peake-Jones |

| | |
|---|---|
| Naylor | Russell Dixon |
| Mr Grubland | Graeme Eton |
| 2nd OAP | Robin Herford |
| 3rd OAP | Marcia Warren |

Directed by Alan Ayckbourn
Musical direction by Paul Todd
Designed by John Hallé

The action takes place in Caroline's flat and various other locations

Time—the present and three years ago

# MUSICAL NUMBERS

## ACT I

| No. | 1 | Overture | Band |
|---|---|---|---|
| No. | 2 | All For Love | Ivor, Jilly, Caroline |
| No. | 3 | Caroline's Questions | Caroline |
| No. | 4 | Montage Sequence | Band |
| No. | 5 | Caroline's Flat | Band |
| No. | 6 | Joanna's Snippet | Joanna |
| No. | 7 | Sanilene | Joanna |
| No. | 8 | Easy Come, Easy Go | Kevin, Joanna, Caroline |
| No. | 9 | Dear Mrs Hughes | Linda |
| No. | 10 | Scene Change | Band |
| No. | 11 | Dorothy And Me | Douglas, Mr Grubland, 2nd and 3rd OAP |
| No. | 12 | Scene Change | Band |
| No. | 13 | Two Can Play | Caroline, Kevin |
| No. | 14 | Scene Change | Band |
| No. | 15 | Table Talk—Part One | Jilly, Joanna, Naylor, Ivor Matthew, Caroline |
| No. | 16 | Table Talk—Part One (Reprise) | Caroline, Matthew |

## ACT II

| No. | 17 | Overture | Band |
|---|---|---|---|
| No. | 18 | Table Talk—Part Two | Jilly, Joanna, Kevin, Caroline, Howard, Ivor |
| No. | 19 | Table Talk—Part Two (Reprise) | Joanna, Kevin |
| No. | 20 | Caroline's Exit | Band |
| No. | 21 | Record Player Music | Band |
| No. | 22 | What Do They Expect? | Caroline, Matthew, Howard Joanna, Kevin |
| No. | 23 | Matthew And Caroline | Band |
| No. | 24 | Montage Sequence | Band |
| No. | 25 | Caroline's Flat | Band |
| No. | 26 | Goodbye | Kevin, Caroline, Anne, Matthew |
| No. | 26A | Goodbye (Reprise) | Band |

| No. 27 | **Scene Change** | Band |
| No. 28 | **Scene Change** | Band |
| No. 29 | **Risking** | Caroline, Matthew |
| No. 30 | **Scene Change** | Band |
| No. 31 | **Scene Change** | Band |
| No. 32 | **Scene Change** | Band |
| No. 33 | **Scene Change** | Band |
| No. 34 | **Individual** | Caroline, Company |
| No. 35 | **Caroline's Answers** (Reprise) | Caroline |

The vocal score is available on hire from Samuel French Ltd

## AUTHOR'S NOTE

The original Scarborough in the round production, designed by John Hallé, was presented on two concentric revolves. An inner 12-foot one served as Caroline's flat and the outer 20 foot for all other locations. Of course, the setting for the play is left entirely to the imagination and discretion of each director and designer. However, it is to be hoped that whatever decision *re* settings they finally reach, they will ensure a fluent and uninterrupted line to the narrative. Ideally, there should be no interruptions or pauses except at the end of each act.

The action throughout alternates between two different periods of time. One, the present, takes place in cold winter just before Christmas. The other, three years earlier, covers early spring and a very hot summer. These changes will be indicated where relevant.

# ACT I

*Caroline's sitting-room. Present time: late Friday afternoon*

### No. 1.   Overture

*The Lights come up on Caroline, in her early thirties, sitting alone in her darkened sitting-room. She is pale and unkempt and has been crying recently. Now she sits emotionless and expressionless in a chair, wearing a dressing-gown and no shoes, a glass in her hand. The room around her, at one time neat, tidy and pleasantly furnished, looks as if a bomb has hit it. It is littered with clothes, papers, books, old cups and saucers, etc.*

*The music ends. The doorbell rings. Caroline does not react. It rings again. A pause*

*We hear the front door being opened with a key. Then voices, Jilly's and Ivor's*

**Jilly** (*off*) There's a mountain of newspapers as well . . .
**Ivor** (*off*) That doesn't look so good . . .
**Jilly** (*off*) Not so good, no . . .
**Ivor** (*off*) Not at all, no . . .

*There is a clink of milk bottles*

I'd better bring some of these in . . .
**Jilly** (*off*) Bring those in, yes. I've got an awful feeling we're going to find her lying here . . .
**Ivor** (*off*) Unconscious . . .
**Jilly** (*off*) Or worse.
**Ivor** (*off*) Or worse.
**Jilly** (*off*) Yes.

*Jilly enters*

(*Switching on the sitting-room lights as she comes in*) I certainly don't . . .

*Caroline blinks but doesn't stir*

*Jilly stands in the doorway. She is smartly dressed, a little older than Caroline. She holds an armful of unread newspapers. She takes in the room and finally Caroline*

Caroline? Caroline, darling . . .? Ivor, she's here.
**Ivor** (*off*) Is she there?
**Jilly** Yes, she's here.
**Ivor** (*off*) Just a minute.

**Jilly** (*moving closer*) Caroline . . .

**Caroline** (*quite brightly if rather drunk*) Oh, hallo.

**Jilly** Thank God. (*Calling to Ivor*) She's alive.

**Ivor** (*off*) Is she alive?

**Jilly** Yes. Caroline, what have you been doing? (*Aware she is holding the newspapers*) Oh. These are yours. (*She puts them down*) I take it you haven't been out in your hall lately.

**Caroline** No, I can't say I have.

**Jilly** We've been worried to death. We even borrowed a key. We thought you'd . . . (*Calling*) Ivor!

**Ivor** (*off*) Coming.

**Jilly** Where are you?

**Ivor** (*off*) I'm just picking up these.

**Jilly** Hurry up. Caroline, where have you been for the past fortnight?

**Caroline** Well, I think I've sort of been sitting here mostly.

**Jilly** All the time?

**Caroline** Most of the time. I had to get up once or twice.

**Jilly** My God, your phone's off the hook. Do you realize your phone is off the hook?

**Caroline** Oh yes, so it is.

**Jilly** (*picking up the instrument*) You could have died. (*She replaces the receiver*)

*As she does so, Ivor, her husband, enters. He is an amiable, unobtrusive sort of man, happy to complement the more forceful Jilly. He is loaded down with a large number of full milk bottles*

**Ivor** Hallo, Caroline.

**Caroline** Hallo, Ivor.

**Ivor** Brought your milk in. Some of it.

**Jilly** He's brought the milk in.

**Ivor** As much as I could anyway.

**Jilly** Look at her, Ivor.

**Ivor** This is a random selection.

**Jilly** Ivor, look at her.

**Ivor** Yes, I am.

**Jilly** Just look.

**Ivor** I am. I'm looking.

**Jilly** What does she look like?

**Ivor** Yes, yes . . .

**Jilly** Make us some tea, Bundle.

**Ivor** Right, I'll make some tea.

*Ivor goes out*

**Jilly** So he really has gone this time, has he?

**Caroline** What?

**Jilly** I said, Kevin really has gone, has he? It's not just another practice bout . . .?

**Caroline** No he's gone. Definitely gone . . .

**Jilly** God, what a mess.

**Caroline** I know. I know I am.

**Jilly** Not you. I meant the room.

**Caroline** Oh. Yes. (*She laughs rather loudly*)

**Jilly** Mind you, come to mention it, you are too . . .

**Caroline** Yes. I've been celebrating.

**Jilly** Good for you. That's surely the right attitude. If he's gone, the bastard's gone.

**Caroline** (*faintly*) Hooray, hooray.

**Jilly** Good riddance. There'll be others.

**Caroline** Boo! Boo!

**Jilly** (*suspiciously*) Have you been drinking? You have, haven't you? (*She takes the glass from Caroline's hand*) God, you reek of gin. How much gin have you drunk?

**Caroline** All of it.

**Jilly** I didn't know you even drank gin.

**Caroline** It's the only stuff that's left. I've drunk everything else, including the brown ale. I was just about to start on the Dabitoff.

*Ivor enters from the kitchen*

**Jilly** Well, we can't go on like this, can we?

**Ivor** Sorry. Bubbles, it's a terrible muddle out here, you know.

**Jilly** Muddle?

**Ivor** Mess. Frightful.

**Jilly** Just make the tea, Bundle.

**Ivor** I was just going to ask Caroline if she'd mind if I did a few things. Cleared up a little. It's just that I can't actually reach the kettle as things are at present.

**Jilly** Yes, Bundle. Just make the tea.

**Ivor** There's a lot of stuff gone off, you see, in there.

**Jilly** Food?

**Ivor** Gone right off. (*To Caroline*) Did you know?

**Caroline** Really? How awful.

**Ivor** Very off.

**Jilly** When did you last go in there?

**Caroline** (*vaguely*) Oh, weeks ago.

**Ivor** There's a sort of green spaghetti bolognese.

**Jilly** Well, throw it away, Bundle.

**Ivor** I'm going to throw it away, Bubbles. It could be er . . .

**Jilly** Dangerous . . .

**Ivor** Health hazard, yes. I'll clear it away.

*Ivor goes out*

**Jilly** (*after him*) Make the tea. (*Returning her attention to Caroline*) Now . . .

*Caroline laughs, lapsing under the next into tears*

(*Acknowledging the laugh*) That's the spirit. What I always say is, if you can only laugh at these things, then you're bound to get a sense of perspec——

*Caroline wails loudly*

Oh, dear God. Caroline, we can't go on like this, can we?

**Caroline** Who cares? Who cares?

**Jilly** Plenty of people. Ivor and I do. For one. Two. And then Howard was asking about you only the other day.

**Caroline** Who the hell's Howard?

**Jilly** You remember Howard. Charming. Rather flabby. He's in soft furnishings . . .

**Caroline** Oh yes. Big, hungry man.

**Jilly** Lovely person. There are lots of others. You'll be so much better off without Kevin. You've no idea . . .

**Caroline** Oh, yes . . .

**Jilly** He was a fool. An utter fool. I said it when you first met him. I said to Ivor: "I'm sorry, Ivor, but she's landed herself with a fool."

**Caroline** You introduced us.

**Jilly** I'm sure I never encouraged you, though. I'd never have encouraged you to marry an actor.

**Caroline** Some people said we were made for each other.

**Jilly** Rubbish. I never said that.

**Caroline** Funny thing is, we were in a way. Made for each other. I think I was made for him and to some extent, Kevin was made for me. Only unfortunately, I think he was made for a lot of other women as well. (*She starts crying*)

**Jilly** Now, Caroline, Caroline. That's enough. You're just feeling sorry for yourself, that's all.

**Caroline** (*wailing*) Yes, I am.

*Ivor enters with a tray of tea things*

**Ivor** This may be a bit on the weak side. You only had one tea bag left, did you know that?

*Caroline sobs*

Ah. (*To Jilly*) Is she . . .?

**Jilly** Take no notice.

**Ivor** Oh yes?

**Jilly** Normal. Normal.

**Ivor** Right, normal. Yes. How do you like your tea, Caroline? Weak or very, very weak? Caroline?

**Caroline** I don't want any.

**Jilly** Give her some.

**Ivor** I don't recommend it. Still . . . (*He pours*)

**Jilly** My God, I see what you mean.

**Ivor** (*proffering a cup*) Caroline?

*Caroline takes it with a sob*

(*To Jilly*) Do you want a cup, Bubbles?
**Jilly** I certainly don't.
**Ivor** No.

*A pause. Caroline sobs and slurps tea*

(*Conversationally*) Jilly's just directed this terrific film, you know, Caroline. It's an industrial film but very good. For this firm that make cardboard boxes. I mean, the subject's not up to much but it's superbly directed. Although I say it myself. Really first rate. I don't know if you can catch it anywhere but . . .

*Caroline sobs*

**Jilly** I don't think she's really interested, Ivor.
**Ivor** No.
**Jilly** Which I suppose places her among the majority of filmgoers . . .

*Caroline carries on crying*

It's best just to let her get it all out.
**Ivor** Yes, yes.
**Jilly** What's happening about your job, Caroline? Aren't the school wondering where you are?
**Caroline** No.
**Jilly** Shouldn't you be there now?
**Caroline** (*recovering a little*) No. I've got—compassionate leave.
**Jilly** Oh, that's good.
**Ivor** Good.
**Caroline** The headmistress told me to take a holiday. She said I was a disturbing influence. "Take a break, Mrs Hughes," she said, "till you're over it."
**Jilly** That was considerate.
**Caroline** She said I was upsetting the girls.
**Ivor** How was that?
**Caroline** I kept crying.
**Jilly** Oh, I see. Well . . .
**Caroline** In Assembly.
**Ivor** Oh dear.
**Caroline** It was the hymns.
**Ivor** The hymns?
**Caroline** They used to set me off. And then the Juniors saw me crying and then they started crying as well. And that started the older girls giggling and the staff started shushing and it was absolute pandemonium. Mass hysteria.
**Jilly** Yes.
**Ivor** Yes.

*Ivor and Jilly are sitting together now on the sofa*

**Caroline** Ivor. Jilly.
**Ivor** Mm?

**Jilly** Yes?

**Caroline** Is it me?

**Jilly** What?

**Caroline** It must be me. Everyone else manages.

**Ivor** Manages what?

**Caroline** Relationships.

**Ivor** Ah. Relationships.

**Jilly** Relationships, Ivor. Do listen, Bundle.

**Ivor** Sorry.

**Caroline** Everyone. You manage. You've made it work . . .

**Jilly** (*smiling a trifle smugly*) Ah well . . .

**Ivor** (*likewise*) Ah . . .

**Jilly** Well some of us are very, very very lucky. Let's face it. You have to allow for luck.

**Ivor** Lucky in love eh? (*He gazes at Jilly adoringly*)

**Jilly** (*gazing back at Ivor*) Mmm . . .

*The music for "All For Love" starts softly*

**Caroline** Yesterday—I think it was yesterday, I had this awful thought . . .

**Jilly** Oh dear, did you? You see, I think the thing about Ivor and me is——

**Ivor** The thing about us——

**Caroline** I had this thought. Perhaps I'm not meant to have a long term meaningful relationship——

**Ivor** Not that there's really any secret——

**Jilly** The point is, you can't class us as being typical. Can she, Bundle?

**Ivor** No, Bubbles, no . . .

**Caroline** I mean the thing is perhaps—perhaps I'm just not meant to be meaningful. Do you see? Do you see what I mean?

*Ivor and Jilly are totally engrossed with each other*

Ivor? Jilly?

**Jilly** Who's a lucky boy then?

**Ivor** Who's a lucky girl?

### No. 2. All For Love

**Jilly**
I married him for love.
I said, why not
I can but try it?

**Ivor**
You need to be in love,
You can't propose
With quid pro quos.
Affairs like those
Will finish in divorce.

*Ivor takes off the tea tray to the kitchen*

**Jilly**
Ivor is a man who's totally himself
He's constantly surprised me.
I would never dream of making any choice
Unless he had advised me.

*Ivor returns from the kitchen*

*He starts to tidy up the room during the next. Jilly assists him a little, mainly by throwing the odd item within reach to Ivor. Caroline, still in her chair, is shifted about when necessary as Ivor scuttles round hither and thither, tidying*

**Ivor**   I leave it all to her,
Sweet Jilly.
That's what she would prefer,
My Jilly—
Little mouse . . .

**Jilly**   Daddy bear . . .

**Ivor**   Don't we make a gorgeous pair?

**Jilly**   Treacle sponge . . .

**Ivor**   Angel pie . . .

**Jilly**   We're so sloppy, he and I.

**Ivor**   I married her for love.
I've no regrets
I still don't doubt it.

**Jilly**   We've based it all on love,
A working team,

**Ivor**   A walking dream,

**Jilly**   To us we seem
The perfect man and wife.

**Ivor**   Jilly is a woman totally herself
So sure of her position.
Here she has a man who's utterly unsure
And lacking in ambition.

**Jilly**   I'd trust him with my life,
Dear Ivor.
He makes a perfect wife,
My Ivor.
Furry fox . . .

**Ivor**   Fleecy lamb . . .

**Jilly**   Guess how much in love I am.

**Ivor**   Coojy-coo . . .

**Jilly**   Kissy-kiss . . .

**Ivor**   We go on for hours like this.

**Ivor** ⎫
**Jilly** ⎭  Besottedly in love—
It feels so good
You can't compare it.

**Caroline**  Oh lucky me—
Happily blessed with such
Dear tender loving friends.

**Jilly**   Belatedly in love.
It's quite absurd
Though take my word
Here's one old bird
Can teach it to the bees.

How I wish
They could be
More aware of me.

**Ivor**   Hide your eyes
Mustn't peak
My turn now for hide and
   seek.

It's good to have such
happy friends.
Why are they saying this
all to me?

| | | |
|---|---|---|
| Jilly | Infant jokes | Won't they stop? |
| | Children's games | I shall scream |
| | Baby talk and stupid names. | Please go home . . . |
| Ivor ⎫ Jilly ⎬ | It's all part of love We don't much mind If we seem silly. | Oh, not again— |
| | | How can they possibly think that |
| | We did it all for love. | I could give a damn? |
| | A doting pair | |
| | Who never care | Oh, dear God, |
| | When people stare | How I hate |
| | And see that we're in love. | Other people's love . . . |

*Ivor moves to the kitchen door laden with junk*

| | |
|---|---|
| Ivor | For we did it— |
| Jilly | Never hid it— |
| Ivor ⎫ Jilly ⎬ | Did it |
| Caroline | All for love. |
| Jilly ⎫ Ivor ⎬ | (*speaking together*) Yes. |

*Ivor goes out*

*The room is now neat and tidy. Caroline looks slightly bemused*

**Jilly** We'll have to go in a second. You must come and have dinner. (*Calling*) Ivor, one minute.

**Ivor** (*off*) One minute, yes. Just finishing here.

**Jilly** He's in his element. We'd stay longer only we've some people coming for a drink. Look, why don't you come to dinner? Tomorrow. Saturday. All right?

**Caroline** (*vaguely*) Tomorrow?

**Jilly** God, you're really in a dreadful state, aren't you?

*Ivor comes out of the kitchen*

**Ivor** That's it. That's done. You could eat a meal off that floor now. Well, you could if you had any food.

**Jilly** Ivor, I've invited Caroline to dinner tomorrow. OK?

**Ivor** Yes, we've got some other people coming but that won't matter, will it?

*The music for "Caroline's Questions" starts*

**Jilly** Not at all. The more the merrier. Now, Caroline, cheer up. You are greatly loved so do not despair.

**Ivor** I'm doing my boeuf en croûte, Caroline.

**Jilly** There, you see. Ivor's doing his en croûte. What greater love . . . ?

**Ivor** Do you like boeuf en croûte?
**Caroline** Yes. I think so.
**Jilly** Lovely. (*Kissing her*) Take care. I'll ring you so keep your phone on the hook, please. Bye.

*Jilly goes out*

**Ivor** (*as he follows*) I could do an avocado surprise. Do you like avocado?
**Caroline** Yes, probably.
**Ivor** Avocado surprise, it is. Bye. That's if I can get avocados, of course.

*Ivor goes out*

*Caroline stands and, after a second's deliberation as she looks round, she comes to a decision—appears to pull herself together and begins to straighten the odd cushion. She pauses for a moment, thoughtfully. Then she sings*

### No. 3.   Caroline's Questions

**Caroline**                    Far too late to ask the question
                                How was I to blame?
                                Am I just a woman who is better off alone?
                                Or perhaps I'm like most teachers
                                Just a kid that's partly grown?
                                Too immature to marry
                                That pathetic female sight
                                Unapproachable by day
                                And so alone at night.

*The Lights change. We are back in past time. The music continues under the following*

*Kevin appears from the front door. He has his jacket on, though it is still obviously a summer night. He is full of excitement. He looks at her. Then he smiles*

(*Speaking*) You got it?
**Kevin** I got it.

*Caroline screams with delight, runs to him and hugs him*

I got the bloody job.
**Caroline**⎤                    ⎡(*excitedly as they embrace*) I said you would. I
           ⎬(*together*)⎨ knew you would. Didn't I say you would?
**Kevin**  ⎦                    ⎣It's absolutely incredible. I can't believe it.
**Caroline** Did you find out the part? What are you playing?
**Kevin** I haven't a clue but he's got eight lines. Who cares?
**Caroline** She said on the phone there were five.
**Kevin** So they're building it up.
**Caroline** And is the money good?
**Kevin** Good? It's got to be good, darling, hasn't it? It's a film for God's sake, a film.

*He goes off removing his jacket to the hall*

*The Lights change back to present time*

**Caroline** (*singing*)  Can I hope to find an answer?
                                    Where did I go wrong?
                                    Should I have the courage to go out and start again?
                                    Have I merely been unlucky with my sorry choice of
                                         men?
                                    Is it they who've been the losers?
                                    Was I wrong or was I right?
                                    I'm uncertain and unsure
                                    And so alone at night . . .

*The music ends. Caroline finds her shoes and puts them on. The phone rings.
Caroline removes it from the hook. The Lights change*

## No. 4.  Montage Sequence

*Caroline slips out of her dressing-gown and picks up a couple of books, as
the sitting-room set clears. She steps forward. We are outside the main
school entrance. Caroline is on her way home*

> *Linda, a girl of about seventeen dressed in school uniform, comes running
> after her bringing Caroline's raincoat*

**Linda** (*breathlessly*)  Miss Baxter! Miss Baxter . . .
**Caroline** (*turning*)  Hallo . . .
**Linda**  Your coat. You left it in the classroom.
**Caroline**  For the eighth time this week. Thank you very much, Linda. I
     don't know what I'd do without you. Would you . . .? (*She hands
     Linda her books as she puts on her coat*)
**Linda**  Miss Baxter . . .
**Caroline**  Yes.
**Linda**  Is there any chance—I hope you don't mind my asking—I was just
     wondering if there was any chance you could give me some extra
     tuition sometime . . .
**Caroline** (*dubiously*)  Oh. Well . . .
**Linda**  After what you've just been saying. It's mainly for English.
**Caroline**  I honestly don't think you need extra tuition, Linda. All you
     need to do is read a bit more. Get a wider background. I gave you that
     supplementary list.
**Linda**  Yes, I know.
**Caroline**  Well, start on that. There's still masses of time.
**Linda**  I just find it easier when there's someone else.
**Caroline**  Ah. Confessions of an undisciplined mind.
**Linda**  Probably.
**Caroline**  I'm not being mean. It's just that the only time I could give you
     extra tuition is after school and I do rather value my evenings. I'm
     never out of this place as it is.

> *Kevin appears, hanging about waiting for Caroline*

*During the following, Caroline sees him and does not hear Linda*

**Linda** (*persistently*)  You see, once I'm able to talk about what I've read

with someone else who understands more than I do, possibly and with
a different viewpoint . . . (*She tails off*)

**Caroline** Hallo.

**Kevin** (*a trifle apologetically*) Me again.

**Caroline** You're making a habit of this, aren't you? Yesterday, now today.

**Kevin** Well, it's on my way. Just in case you needed me to carry your
books again.

**Caroline** I see. (*Aware of Linda*) Oh, this is Linda. Linda, this is Mr
Hughes—Kevin.

**Linda** Hallo.

**Kevin** (*barely glancing at her*) Hi. (*To Caroline*) Well, are you set?

**Caroline** Right. Good-night then, Linda.

**Linda** Good-night, Miss Baxter.

*Linda moves away rather reluctantly and exits*

*Kevin and Caroline walk a few paces*

**Caroline** This isn't out of your way, is it?

**Kevin** No.

**Caroline** Are you on your way back?

**Kevin** Back where?

**Caroline** Back from work.

**Kevin** No.

**Caroline** Oh.

**Kevin** I'm not actually working just at the moment.

**Caroline** Oh, I see. It's what you actors call resting, is it?

**Kevin** No. It's what we actors call unemployed, actually.

**Caroline** Oh. Does it depress you? Not working?

**Kevin** No.

**Caroline** Ah.

**Kevin** Yes. Very much. That's why I've walked a mile and a half to meet
you. Because otherwise I'd have been even more depressed. Fortunately
since we met at Jilly's the day before yesterday, things have been perking
up. Because I've met a very attractive, very lovely person who might do
me the world of good.

**Caroline** How nicely put. Thank you. You may carry my books.

**Kevin** My pleasure.

*The Lights change. The music peaks as the scene changes to a restaurant
table, inexpensive but intimate. They sit. They have just finished a meal*

You can't keep on buying me meals . . .

**Caroline** Why not?

**Kevin** Well . . .

**Caroline** Is it offending your male principles?

**Kevin** Just my principles. I wouldn't like it any more if you were a man
who kept buying me meals.

**Caroline** If I were a man, I don't think I'd bother. That was nice, that. I
don't think I've ever had Tyrolean food.

**Kevin** I doubt if the chef has either.

**Caroline** How do you know?

**Kevin** He was at drama school with me. He's Welsh.

**Caroline** My God, I'm keeping your friends as well.

**Kevin** You know, you're a very funny mixture.

**Caroline** Me?

**Kevin** Well, half of you's very old fashioned and the other half's very— pow . . .

**Caroline** Old fashioned?

**Kevin** A bit. It's a nice quality.

**Caroline** Is it? I'm not so sure.

**Kevin** It's just your manner sometimes. Not in bed. I don't mean in bed.

**Caroline** Oh. What's my manner in bed?

**Kevin** Oh, definitely pow.

**Caroline** Ah.

*Caroline and Kevin get up from the table. As they do so, the music peaks and changes*

> *Kevin exits*

> *The Lights also cross to reveal Linda, standing in a classroom, holding a gift-wrapped parcel*

**Linda** (*rather nervously*) On behalf of all of us in Five A, we would like to congratulate you very much, Miss Baxter, on your engagement. And we would like you very much to accept this small gift as a token of our good wishes.

**Caroline** Well. Wow. Thank you very much. I'm very touched. Thank you. All of you. (*Very confused*) I don't know what to say.

> *Caroline and Linda exit*

*The music peaks and changes as the Lights cross fade to Caroline's sitting-room. It is clean, bright and sunlit*

> *Kevin enters and goes and sprawls with his feet on the sofa*

> *Caroline enters, carrying her present still wrapped*

**Kevin** What's that?

**Caroline** Something the girls gave me. Us. An engagement present.

**Kevin** Oh.

**Caroline** I haven't had a minute to open it. I thought you might meet me. Did you go for the interview?

**Kevin** Yep.

**Caroline** Any hope?

**Kevin** They didn't want to know. I got halfway through the first piece. Thank you so much, good-afternoon. Bastards. It was all rigged.

**Caroline** (*opening her present*) Oh that's nice.

**Kevin** What?

**Caroline** It's a book of love poems.

**Kevin** Oh, very kinky.

**Caroline** No, it's not. It's very nice. (*She reads the inscription inside*) Oh, that's lovely . . .

**Kevin** What do they think about us at the school?
**Caroline** How do you mean?
**Kevin** Living together.
**Caroline** You mean, the girls?
**Kevin** Do they know?
**Caroline** Well, I haven't told them but they're not stupid.
**Kevin** What about your colleagues? What do they say?
**Caroline** They don't. I don't think they mind. Providing I don't get up and actually announce it during Assembly. By the way, school, I am having it away with Mr Hughes every evening so please, could I ask you to have all your English compositions on my desk in good time . . . What's the matter?
**Kevin** Nothing.
**Caroline** Anything I can do?
**Kevin** No.
**Caroline** You still want to go through with this?
**Kevin** What?
**Caroline** The marriage. Us. All that.
**Kevin** Of course.
**Caroline** That isn't what's depressing you?
**Kevin** No. I want to marry you.
**Caroline** Good.
**Kevin** On our terms that is.
**Caroline** Oh yes.
**Kevin** Total freedom still to be ourselves.
**Caroline** Right.
**Kevin** You want to go your way, you go your way. It's up to you.
**Caroline** Super, yes.
**Kevin** And the same for me.
**Caroline** Oh yes.
**Kevin** As long as it's agreed.
**Caroline** Yes, we agreed.
**Kevin** Fine.

*He sees she is troubled*

   What's the matter?
**Caroline** Sorry. Do you think you could just get your shoes off the sofa, do you think, love?
**Kevin** Oh, right.

*The music peaks and the Lights cross fade to a school corridor*

   *Kevin exits*

   *Miss Dent enters*

*Caroline, moving hurriedly between classes, passes Miss Dent, a teacher in her mid-forties, also changing classes*

**Miss Dent** Oh Caroline, I meant to say before, congratulations.

**Caroline** Thank you, Miss Dent.

**Miss Dent** Absolutely flabbergasted us all. We had no idea you were taking the plunge. You didn't seem the type.

**Caroline** Really? Well . . .

**Miss Dent** With an actor, I understand.

**Caroline** Yes.

**Miss Dent** Jolly good. Splendid. That'll be a challenge. Yes. I think we all had you marked down as an old bachelor.

**Caroline** Oh, did you? I wasn't actually contemplating a sex-change, Miss Dent.

**Miss Dent** (*laughing heartily*) Well, I've got a geog. class. I hope you and your actor are very, very happy. And may you take many, many curtain calls together. Bye.

*Miss Dent hurries away*

*The music peaks and changes to very loud, party/disco type music. The Lights cross fade*

> *Kevin and Joanna enter and stand together, both holding glasses. She is an attractive, rather glossy woman in her mid-twenties*

*Throughout the next, there is the sound of everyone shouting to each other above the din*

**Kevin** (*waving*) Darling . . .

*He waves Caroline over to them. She moves closer*

**Caroline** Sorry. I was talking to . . .

**Kevin** Have you met Joanna?

**Joanna** Hallo.

**Caroline** How do you do.

**Kevin** Joanna, this is my wife as of this morning.

**Joanna** Congratulations.

**Caroline** Thank you. (*To Kevin*) This music's terribly loud, darling.

**Kevin** We want it loud, it's a party.

**Caroline** Oh. Just getting a headache.

**Joanna** We were all just saying we loathe you.

**Caroline** What?

**Joanna** We all hate you for taking Kevin out of circulation. It's most unfair.

**Caroline** Ah.

**Kevin** I'll get you both another drink.

**Joanna** Thank you.

*Kevin exits*

**Caroline** Kev, could . . . (*She sees Kevin has gone*)

**Joanna** Super party.

**Caroline** Very loud.

**Joanna** Yes, super. Sorry, don't be offended, will you, but I do think it's absolutely hysterical Kevin marrying a schoolteacher. Absolutely hysterical.

**Caroline** Why's that?

**Joanna** Well, no reflection on you, but that man finishing up with a schoolteacher is a bit like Evel Knievel marrying a traffic warden. Still I can thoroughly recommend him. He's absolutely sensational in all departments. Or have you already found that out?

**Caroline** Yes, excuse me, I must just . . .

**Joanna** (*moving away*) Yes, don't mind me. See you.

*Joanna goes*

*Caroline stands scowling for a moment. The party music swells. The Lights cross fade to the sitting-room. Only now we are back in present time and it is gloomily lit as before. The music finishes. Caroline stands in the middle of the room. The doorbell rings. She stands. It rings again*

**Caroline** Oh hell.

*She pulls on her dressing-gown and goes to answer the front door. She returns with Miss Dent, now well wrapped up in winter garb*

**Miss Dent** . . . thank you so much. It is very cold, isn't it?

**Caroline** Yes, I haven't been out today yet but . . .

**Miss Dent** Oh well, wrap up warm when you do. I think it's going to snow. Sorry, have I caught you at a wrong time?

**Caroline** No. I'm sorry about the . . . Please, do sit down.

**Miss Dent** Thank you. Oh, for you . . . (*She hands Caroline a box of chocolates*)

**Caroline** Oh.

**Miss Dent** Nothing. Just a little . . .

**Caroline** Thank you. Can I offer you anything?

**Miss Dent** Well, um . . .

**Caroline** Actually I'm sorry, on second thoughts I don't think I've got anything to offer you.

**Miss Dent** Ah.

**Caroline** Sorry. (*Proffering the chocolates*) Unless you'd like . . .

**Miss Dent** Well, maybe just one.

**Caroline** Please, go ahead.

**Miss Dent** (*taking the box*) It's naughty, I shouldn't. They're very bad for me. Thank you. Really, all I wanted to say—the reason I came round . . . (*Offering the box*) Will you?

**Caroline** Not just at the moment.

**Miss Dent** They're really quite nice . . . What I wanted to say was how awfully sorry I am that things haven't worked out for you.

**Caroline** Oh well . . .

**Miss Dent** I do understand. I really do.

**Caroline** Thank you.

**Miss Dent** You look very shattered.

**Caroline** Do I?

**Miss Dent** You've obviously been crying.

**Caroline** Oh yes. Well, it has been rather grim, I suppose, with all the circumstances. I'm just sorry the school's been involved.

**Miss Dent** I don't think it's the school. I don't think you can blame the school.

**Caroline** No, I didn't mean that.

**Miss Dent** Not that I'm defending it purely as deputy-headmistress. But I've been there twenty years and I was a pupil before that.

**Caroline** Yes, I realize.

**Miss Dent** No, I don't think you can blame the school for one bad apple. She was an evil girl, I admit it, very evil.

**Caroline** I wouldn't say that. She's very young and——

**Miss Dent** I know evil, Mrs Hughes. I've seen it many times and I recognize it.

**Caroline** Well . . .

**Miss Dent** Do you mind my calling you Mrs Hughes? Or would you prefer your maiden name?

**Caroline** No, I'm still married. Technically anyway.

**Miss Dent** I did.

**Caroline** I'm sorry?

**Miss Dent** I changed my name back.

**Caroline** Oh, I see. I'm sorry, I had no idea you——

**Miss Dent** Oh yes. I was married for a short while. Long, long, long time ago. Very briefly. He was taken from me.

**Caroline** Your husband was?

**Miss Dent** Yes.

**Caroline** Was this in the war?

**Miss Dent** The war?

**Caroline** Was he killed in action?

**Miss Dent** Certainly not. How old do you think I am, for heaven's sake?

**Caroline** Oh yes, of course.

**Miss Dent** I'm only forty-six, you know.

**Caroline** I'm sorry.

**Miss Dent** I mean, I may seem ancient to you . . .

**Caroline** No, no.

**Miss Dent** One can see you don't teach history.

**Caroline** It's just when you said your husband was taken from you, I thought . . .

**Miss Dent** He was taken from me, under the same circumstances as yours. By another woman.

**Caroline** Oh, I see.

**Miss Dent** So I feel somehow very personally involved, Miss Baxter—Caroline. May I? Caroline?

**Caroline** Yes. Look, Miss Dent, I don't really think I want——

**Miss Dent** Candida. Please call me Candida.

**Caroline** Yes, of course.

**Miss Dent** (*warming up*) I don't know if you've ever felt, Caroline, that things like this were meant . . . (*She helps herself to another chocolate. By the end of the scene, she has eaten most of the box*) That one can spend over twenty-five years of loneliness apparently to no purpose. And then find suddenly, after all, it was intended. Do you see?

**Caroline** I think so . . . I'm not sure I——

**Miss Dent** I was very, very young when I met Adam. We were younger than you are. We were so happy.

### No. 5.   Caroline's Flat

*The Lights change slowly to past time on a summer evening*

*Kevin enters from the kitchen and stands in the doorway drinking beer from a can. During the next he sits on the sofa and puts his feet up*

I don't think it's possible to analyse happiness. I've often tried. But it's very elusive and intangible, isn't it? Certainly Adam and I experienced it.

*The music cuts off*

**Caroline** Kevin, for the last time, will you please get your feet off that——

**Kevin** OK. (*He takes his feet off the sofa*)

**Caroline** Thank you.

**Kevin** Our sofa. This end's mine.

**Miss Dent** I'm not boring you?

**Caroline** Oh, no.

**Kevin** I think you should've married this sofa, you know.

**Caroline** I'm sorry.

**Kevin** You both hate me.

**Caroline** Did you have a nice day?

**Kevin** It was OK. One doesn't really expect to experience a sense of acute artistic satisfaction whilst filming a thirty second TV commercial for a lavatory cleanser but at least I was working and getting paid and after eight months, that is a great step forward.

**Caroline** I was thinking, just temporarily, to help out, I might do a little extra tuition. In the evenings. Some of the girls were asking.

**Kevin** Evenings?

**Caroline** Just for a couple of hours. Only till you're earning again.

**Kevin** Hardly see you anyway.

**Caroline** Two days a week.

**Kevin** There goes our social life.

**Caroline** Social life?

**Kevin** You're working all week and every weekend you're with your father.

**Caroline** Saturday afternoons I'm with my father, that's all. Why don't you come with me?

**Kevin** No, thank you. I can think of better ways of spending my weekend than listening to the half-baked, philosophical utterances of a reactionary tobacconist.

**Caroline** Thank you. I'm very fond of your mother too.

**Miss Dent** I think it was the sensation of feeling so unclean. That a relationship that has started with so much spiritual cleanliness should be soiled by her. It was, you know. It was soiled.

**Kevin** I'll tell you who I saw today. Sent her love.

**Caroline** Who's that?

**Kevin** She was working on this commercial with me. Had the odd line. Joanna. Do you remember Joanna?

**Caroline** (*vaguely*) Er . . .

**Kevin** You met her at our party. Our wedding reception. Whatever we called it.

*The music for "Joanna's Snippet" starts*

**Caroline** Oh yes. Joanna.

*Joanna appears, separate from them, in a solo light. She sings*

### No. 6.   Joanna's Snippet

**Joanna**               So you're the one who's caught him at last.
                         It really is most unfair
                         That you've tied down this fabulous man
                         Whom all of us want to share.

*Joanna exits*

**Kevin** Sent her love.

**Caroline** Oh good.

**Kevin** She brightened things up a bit, anyway. I mean, she's a lousy actress. She'll never play Hedda Gabler but she's a good laugh. Come to think of it, she'd probably be quite good as Hedda Gabler.

**Caroline** Yes, I found her very witty.

**Kevin** Yes.

**Caroline** Had me rolling around in stitches.

**Kevin** (*scowling*) All right. All right.

**Miss Dent** . . . I think I temporarily lost my sanity. I must have done. I destroyed everything of his I could find. I smashed and tore up everything. Everything of his that I knew he valued. It's frightening to feel that you have that sort of fury inside you, isn't it . . . ?

*Joanna appears again, in her solo light as before, now dressed as a lavatory brush. She sings*

### No. 7.   Sanilene

**Joanna**               If you want Elizabeth Brush
                         To polish your toilet clean
                         She'll require some regular help
                         From wonderful Sanilene.

*Joanna goes off*

**Miss Dent** (*rising*) I must go. I'm taking up far too much of your time.

**Caroline** No.

**Kevin** I hope you're not turning into the cliché wife.

**Miss Dent** Goodbye.

**Kevin** Standing at the door with a rolling-pin.
**Caroline** Don't be silly.
**Miss Dent** I'm afraid I've eaten all these.
**Caroline** It doesn't matter.
**Kevin** Or I'll turn into the cliché husband.
**Caroline** Please don't.
**Miss Dent** (*going*) Goodbye.

*She goes out*

**Caroline** Goodbye.
**Kevin** Hey.
**Caroline** What?
**Kevin** I said hey. Dreamer.
**Caroline** Sorry. I was just thinking. It's such an art, isn't it? Living with someone? There's so much—adjustment—needed.
**Kevin** Not necessarily.
**Caroline** Obviously.
**Kevin** Why change because I'm here?
**Caroline** I have to.
**Kevin** Why?
**Caroline** Because you *are* here.
**Kevin** I don't see why. I don't alter because you're here.
**Caroline** No. No, I don't think you do much, do you?
**Kevin** I'm me.
**Caroline** Yes, I know.
**Kevin** That's what you wanted. That's what you've got . . . (*He sings*)

### No. 8.   Easy Come, Easy Go

Love's no love that seeks to restrain you.
Home's no home that tries to contain you.
As we are.
Let us be.
You be you
I'll be me.

Marriages
From the start
Change your name
Then your heart.

Life requires
Ebb and flow.
Easy come,
Easy go.

Our wedding was lovers' leap
With this ring I'll with thee sleep
Love never came more cheap.

This despite our solemn intention
Not to live by dreary convention.
How could we
Calmly vow
What we'd feel
Years from now?

Picture you
Way ahead
Stuck with me
Till you're dead.
Life's too long
We both know.
Easy come,
Easy go.

There's nothing that I could sign.
Documents cannot define
Love that's as free as mine.

*Joanna enters and sings*

| | |
|---|---|
| **Joanna** | Here she comes, Elizabeth Brush, |
| | The lavatory-cleansing queen. |
| | Creeping through your bedroom door |
| | And picking your marriage clean. |
| | I'm here to add fresh excitement to his life |
| | Can you face the opposition? |
| | Bear the competition? |
| | Can you be sure, once a man has seen the stars, |
| | He will give up all ambition? |
| | Resume his old position? |
| **Kevin** | Lock man up, you're certain to lose him—— |
| **Joanna** | Lay down rules you'll only confuse him—— |
| **Kevin** | Set him free—— |
| **Joanna** | Leave him spare . . . |
| **Kevin** | Free to give . . . |
| **Joanna** | Free to share . . . |
| **Kevin** | Love's for all |
| | Not for some—— |
| **Joanna** | Easy go, |
| | Easy come . . . |
| | Man's a cock |
| | Needs to crow . . . |
| **Kevin** | Easy come, |
| | Easy go. |
| **Joanna** | I hope this won't sound unkind, |
| **Caroline** | Meow. |

| | |
|---|---|
| **Joanna** | Marriage for women, I find, |
| **Caroline** | Meow. |
| **Joanna** | Tends to destroy their mind . . . |

*Joanna exits*

| | |
|---|---|
| **Caroline** | Please rush off if you feel the need to, |
| | Don't feel bound by all we've agreed to. |
| | What's an oath |
| | Here or there? |
| | Easy vow, |
| | Easy swear. |
| | |
| | Off you go |
| | Glad you came. |
| | There's your coat. |
| | Take your name. |
| **Kevin** | Love's a light |
| | Needs to glow—— |
| **Caroline** | Overload |
| | Fuses blow . . . |
| **Kevin** | It's tragic you can't adjust |
| **Caroline** | What you call love I call lust . . . |
| **Kevin** | Whatever came of trust? |
| | Why not live the way that we planned to? |
| **Caroline** | Here's one wife who does understand you. |
| **Kevin** | As we are |
| | We will be—— |
| **Caroline** | More of you |
| | Less of me |
| **Kevin** | Love's a dance, |
| | To and fro, |
| **Caroline** | One false step |
| | One less toe. |
| **Both** | Easy come, |
| | Easy go. |
| **Kevin** | Here it comes . . . |
| **Caroline** | There it all goes. |

*Kevin exits at the end of the song*

*The Lights change to Caroline's kitchen. It is past time: a hot summer evening*

*Caroline starts to clear the odd thing off the table and lay it with a cloth*

*Kevin enters as she is doing this*

**Kevin** What are you doing?
**Caroline** I'm just trying to make this a bit more pleasant to work at.
**Kevin** Work?
**Caroline** It's Thursday. It's Linda's evening for extra tuition.

**Kevin** Oh God, again.

**Caroline** Look, I've moved in here. I can't do any more. I've left you the sitting-room so you can watch your telly. I don't particularly want to sit in a kitchen.

**Kevin** OK.

**Caroline** I'm not doing it for fun. It's not my idea of how to spend an evening.

**Kevin** I said nothing. (*He helps himself to a can of beer from the fridge*)

**Caroline** I mean, I think I'm being bloody reasonable. Sitting out here . . .

**Kevin** Yes.

**Caroline** Just so you can watch television.

**Kevin** I need to watch television for my work. It's my job.

**Caroline** I don't see how.

**Kevin** Because it helps if I go and meet the director afterwards, that's why.

**Caroline** But you only watch old films. Half those directors are dead.

**Kevin** I'm not arguing. You know nothing about showbusiness.

**Caroline** That makes two of us.

**Kevin** You're not reasonable tonight.

**Caroline** Kevin, I'm sick to death of doing everything. I finish work, I get home, then I have to start again here.

**Kevin** Well, don't.

**Caroline** Someone has to, darling.

*The doorbell rings*

(*Moving*) That'll be Linda.

**Kevin** I'll go.

**Caroline** It's all right.

**Kevin** I'll go.

**Caroline** (*going*) I can manage.

*She goes out*

**Kevin** (*to himself*) God. (*He whistles a snatch of "Easy Come, Easy Go" whilst helping himself to several cans of beer from the fridge*)

*Caroline returns with Linda who is carrying a bag*

**Caroline** I'm afraid we're in here tonight, Linda. I hope that's all right. My husband has to do some work. You've met Linda, haven't you, Kevin?

**Kevin** No.

**Linda** Yes, we have, I think.

**Kevin** Have we? Great. Right, I'll leave you to it. (*He gathers up his cans*)

**Caroline** Thank you. Light refreshment?

**Kevin** Yes.

**Caroline** Lovely. Darling, if you could remember, whilst you're researching, to keep the volume turned down, I'd be very grateful.

**Kevin** Do my best, my love. See you later.

*Kevin goes out*

*Caroline is still very angry. She takes a deep breath to control this. Linda watches her intently*

**Caroline** Right. Sit down, Linda.

**Linda** It's a lovely kitchen.

**Caroline** Thank you. It's . . .

**Linda** Are you a very good cook, Mrs Hughes?

**Caroline** Well, no, not awfully good. I do basics quite well. Roasts and stews and things and I make a very good spaghetti bolognese but I'm nothing special.

**Linda** I think those sort of things are often the most difficult. The basics.

**Caroline** Yes. Anyway, sit down, Linda.

**Linda** I think it's a lovely kitchen.

**Caroline** Yes. Well, it's just a fairly ordinary old kitchen really. You better sit down, you're paying for this. Or your parents are. So you better get your money's worth. Is that chair all right?

**Linda** It's lovely.

**Caroline** (*sorting through text books and exercise books*) Now, we'd better get back to *Comus*, I suppose. (*Searching for a book*) Where did we get to, do you remember? Don't say I haven't got it. Oh no, just a second. I've left *Comus* in the other room.

**Linda** It's all right, Mrs Hughes, there's this one. I've got this one.

**Caroline** Oh, all right. Perhaps we'd better not disturb my husband's studies. (*Taking the book from her*) Where did we get to? Round about line two-twenty or two-thirty, I think. We hadn't got to Chastity yet, had we?

**Linda** No.

**Caroline** No—whoops. (*A piece of paper falls from the book. She picks it up and glances at it briefly*) No, I think we'd got to Echo. "Sweet Echo, sweetest nymph . . ." Back to the nymphs again. He's—what's this?

**Linda** Nothing.

**Caroline** What is it?

**Linda** Nothing. Could I have it, please?

**Caroline** Yes, of course. Sorry. None of my business. (*She hands the paper over*)

**Linda** (*taking it*) Thank you.

**Caroline** Warm in here.

**Linda** Yes.

**Caroline** "Sweet Echo, sweetest nymph that liv'st unseen
　　　Within thy airy shell
　　　By slow . . ."

**Linda** It's a poem.

**Caroline** Well, yes. A poetic masque. But, of course, Milton always . . .

**Linda** I meant, this was. (*Indicating the paper*) Here.

**Caroline** Oh. That. (*Puzzled*) About me?

**Linda** Yes.

**Caroline** Who by? You?

**Linda** Yes.

**Caroline** Oh, how nice. I'm flattered. I hope.

**Linda** I'd like you to read it.

**Caroline** Well, I . . . Oh, all right. If you'd like me to. (*Taking the paper*)
I'm afraid I can't give you any marks for it. (*She laughs*)

*The music for "Dear Mrs Hughes" starts*

*Caroline reads a few lines. After a second, she folds the paper and hands it
back to Linda*

I don't think I really ought to be reading that, Linda.
**Linda** Please.
**Caroline** (*gently*) No, honestly, I don't think I should. Thank you, I'm
very touched.
**Linda** Then I'll read it. I'll read it.
**Caroline** (*ineffectually*) Linda . . .

### No. 9.   Dear Mrs Hughes

**Linda** (*singing*)      Most of the
                          Girls at school
                          Gawp at TV
                          Worshipping groups that do
                          Nothing for me.
                          If they should
                          Ever ask
                          Who would I choose
                          It would be fabulous
                          You, Mrs Hughes.
                          I admire
                          Someone with
                          Inner repose,
                          Someone with confidence
                          Someone who knows.
                          How I wish
                          That I could
                          Stand in your shoes,
                          Just for a second be
                          You, Mrs Hughes.
                          Somebody I'd give my life to serve
                          So grateful that I'm with them.
                          Every little wish is my command
                          Behold your slave
                          Ever more,
                          Mrs Hughes,
                          I'm yours.
                          I've found a meaning to my life
                              that I never had
                          Learnt things I'd never hope to learn
                              from my mum and my dad.
                          Till I met you.

**Caroline** (*reading*) "Where the lovelorn nightingale
                        Nightly to thee her sad song mourneth well . . ."
**Linda**                   Laugh at me
                            If you wish
                            What do I care?
                            This is a secret that
                            Only I share.
                            One thing I beg of you,
                            Please don't refuse,
                            Can I call you Caroline,
                            Dear Mrs Hughes?
                            Here's my heart and here's my soul
                            I'm yours to do your bidding,
                            Caroline, you have to see
                            That it's no use
                            It's the truth
                            It is you
                            I love.
                            If you should turn me down
                            What can I lose?
                            I shall just kill myself,
                            Dear Mrs Hughes.

*Linda sits. An embarrassed pause*

**Caroline** Linda . . . I—what am I to say? I mean, I don't . . . I've never . . .
I'm really most—I've—I'm . . . (*She laughs rather hysterically. Pulling
herself together*) I'm sorry, no, I'm not laughing. I'm just rather embarrassed. There's no reason to be but . . . (*She laughs again*)

*Linda gets up quickly, very hurt. She snatches up her belongings, leaving
behind only her copy of Milton and runs out*

I'm sorry. Linda, I'm sorry. I didn't—oh, dear God, I'm not actually
laughing, Linda. Well, not at you. I'm just . . . Linda!

*Linda has gone*

*Kevin comes in*

**Kevin** What's happened? What's the matter?
**Caroline** Oh dear.
**Kevin** What?
**Caroline** (*going out after Linda*) Nothing. It's nothing you'd possibly
understand.

*Caroline exits*

**Kevin** I see. (*He picks up the Milton and opens it at random. He reads*)
    " . . . a hidden strength
        Which, if heav'n gave it, may be term'd her own:
        'Tis chastity, my brother, chastity.

> She that has that is clad in complete steel,
> And like——"
> My God, what is she teaching them?

### No. 10.  Scene Change

*Kevin goes out*

*The Lights cross fade. It is present time. The scene changes to Douglas Baxter's shop, a tobacconist's and newsagent's*

> *Douglas enters. He is a man in his sixties*

> *Caroline comes through from the back of the shop with a cup of tea*

**Caroline**  Here you are, Dad. There's two sugars.

**Douglas**  Thank you, Carol.

**Caroline**  (*murmuring*) Caroline, Dad.

**Douglas**  I haven't seen you for a fortnight. Been neglected. You staying on for dinner?

**Caroline**  No, I'm afraid not, Dad. I've been invited out.

**Douglas**  Ah-ha.

**Caroline**  Just Jilly and Ivor. Nothing fantastic. They probably want me to make up numbers. Spare female.

**Douglas**  They're inviting you because they want your company. That's why they're inviting you. You're looking better.

**Caroline**  Am I? Good.

**Douglas**  Now, I'm glad you're not letting this get on top of you, Carol. That means we taught you something. I always said to you, people can sometimes let you down but you needn't let them get on top of you. If we've taught you that, we've taught you something. Your mother's a fighter. I'm a fighter.

**Caroline**  Have you heard from Mum?

**Douglas**  She phoned on Thursday. She's very well. I think the sea air's beginning to bring an improvement.

**Caroline**  How much longer is she going to be there?

**Douglas**  Till she's right in herself.

**Caroline**  It must be costing you a fortune, keeping her in that hotel.

**Douglas**  I've got nothing else to spend it on, have I? Me and Buster, that's all. Tin of baked beans and a couple of tins of dog food sees us through. I'm happy if I can feel your mother's on the mend. Dorothy's all that concerns me. That's what it's all about. Caring. That's what's missing, you see. Your Kevin—nice lad—but there was no caring in him. He was devoid of caring.

**Caroline**  Yes, OK, Dad. Maybe I wasn't worth caring that much about.

**Douglas**  Now, now, don't you run yourself down again, I won't have that.

*The shop bell sounds*

> That's no way for a daughter of mine to behave.

> *Mr Grubland, an OAP, comes in. He is an old man*

> Good-afternoon, Mr Grubland. How are we today?

**Mr Grubland** All right.

**Douglas** Good, good.

**Mr Grubland** Have a look through, can I?

**Douglas** Help yourself, Mr Grubland. Have a look through. (*To Caroline*) He looks through all the mags, you know, every week. All he ever has is his *Radio Times*.

**Caroline** The point is, Dad, I was brought up by you to believe that it takes two to make a relationship.

**Douglas** True. True.

**Caroline** It also takes two to destroy one. If Kev's gone off, OK, maybe he was a bastard . . . Sorry, maybe he was unreliable but it may also be that there's something lacking in me.

**Douglas** All right there, Mr Grubland, are you?

**Mr Grubland** Yes.

**Caroline** Do you see?

**Douglas** I don't know what you're talking about, girl. Your mother and I brought you up the best way we could. You lacked for absolutely nothing. And, believe me, in those days that meant we went without a lot.

**Caroline** Yes, I know.

**Douglas** Now, you turn round and tell me there's something lacking.

**Caroline** I didn't mean that.

**Douglas** We did what we could, Caroline. If you'd seen your mother's hands . . .

**Caroline** (*screaming*) I didn't mean that——(*She checks herself*) Sorry.

**Douglas** No, I won't have you shouting in the shop, Carol. I won't have shouting or swearing in my shop.

**Caroline** I wasn't swearing.

**Douglas** That's the only rule.

**Caroline** Where did I go wrong? You saw us together. Please, tell me. What did I do wrong?

**Douglas** The only thing wrong with you, girl—excuse me, Mr Grubland, I'm just putting my daughter straight—the only thing wrong with you, Carol, is you spend too much time thinking and worrying about yourself. Get some perspective. See things from the other point of view occasionally. Look through the eyes of others. And, above all, look on the bright side. Just remember this, you can often waste your words but a smile is never wasted.

**Caroline** How true.

**Douglas** Look at me and your mother. The problems we had to cope with but we overcame them. We tackled them together. Thick and thin. Better or worse. (*He sings*)

### No. 11.  Dorothy and Me

No, it never rained in those days
Only pennies from the sky
And a penny then was worth a fortune

Though we'd not a ha'penny, she and I
And despite the fact it was wartime
We got by . . .
When me and Dorothy were young
We had no troubles like the ones they have today.
We simply met and fell in love
And listen . . .
Those church bells were ringing——
Silver threads and gold
Me and my girl have now grown old together——
Happy still to be
Dorothy and me.
When me and Mrs B. were young
We faced our worries with a whistle and a grin
We packed our troubles up and smiled
In kitbags
Said bye-bye to blackbirds.
Knew those clouds of grey
Would somewhere have a silver lining to them
We'd be bound to see
Dorothy and me.

*Mr Grubland is joined by the 2nd and 3rd OAP who harmonize under the next*

There were bluebirds down in Dover
You could hear the rabbits run
All the little lambs were eating ivy
For the doodle-bugs had just begun
Even though we had no bananas
We had fun.
When me and Dorothy were young
We had our moments when we said *auf Wiedersehen*
We knew some day we'd meet again
Keep smiling
And digging—for victory
Kiss the boys goodbye
It's going to be a lovely day tomorrow
Rose of Picardy
Dorothy and me.

*Douglas and the OAPs repeat the last verse*

*Everyone exits at the end of the song*

## No. 12.  Scene Change

*The scene changes back to Caroline's sitting-room. It is past time: evening*

*Kevin comes on. He is finishing dressing, ready to go out*

**Kevin**  I don't know what you're talking about.

**Caroline** (*off*) You know.

**Kevin** No idea. What was I supposed to do? (*No reply*) Did you want the place spring cleaning, did you? While you were out? You should have said so. I'd've done it with pleasure. I don't charge a lot. You'll find my rates extremely reasonable. Unemployed actors cheapest form of sweated labour. A bit of pocket money, that's all I ask. Just something to tide me over for three or four years until I get a job . . .

*Caroline enters in a slip*

**Caroline** Whose fault's that?

**Kevin** Hardly mine.

**Caroline** You've given up looking, haven't you?

*Caroline goes off the other way to collect her dress*

**Kevin** I was out last week.

**Caroline** (*off*) For half an hour. And then you got drunk.

**Kevin** With an agent. Can I help it if he was an alcoholic? I was with the agent.

*Caroline returns holding her dress*

**Caroline** (*as she comes in*) So you said.

**Kevin** What do you mean by that? (*He stands and blocks her path*)

**Caroline** (*trying to pass him*) Excuse me.

**Kevin** No, come on. What did that mean—"So you said"?

**Caroline** Nothing.

**Kevin** No, it meant something. Are you suggesting I'm a liar? That I was lying to you?

**Caroline** I didn't say that.

**Kevin** Well, that was your implication. I will have you know I have never lied to you. Never. And I never will do.

**Caroline** I'm not interested at the moment, Kevin. I'm really not. I just want to get dressed.

**Kevin** You can get dressed when I've finished.

**Caroline** Would you get out of my way, please?

**Kevin** When I've finished talking to you, yes.

**Caroline** Kevin, we are going to be late.

**Kevin** I don't care.

**Caroline** Well, I do. Jilly and Ivor are expecting us at seven-thirty.

**Kevin** I'm not interested.

**Caroline** I am not going to ruin their evening.

**Kevin** I'm not interested. I want to know why you suddenly attacked me.

**Caroline** (*exploding*) My God. I come back here this evening having spent the whole afternoon cleaning my bloody parents' house because my mother has grandly decided to spend the rest of her days in a hotel in Bournemouth and my father is too mean to get anyone in to clean it for him and too poor anyway because he has to send all the money he has to my mother . . .

**Kevin** All right, all right.

**Caroline** Let me finish. And I come home here at six o'clock in the evening, absolutely exhausted because I also happen to have been doing exams all week and I find the place in a tip and you're in bed reading and burning holes in my sheets——

**Kevin** Our sheets.

**Caroline** No, Kevin. Enough is enough. They are my sheets. This is my flat and my furniture and my sheets. The only thing in this place which is yours is the rubbish. Now, get out of my way.

*Kevin does so. Caroline is a little surprised. Kevin picks up a few objects and drops them on the floor*

**Kevin** These are all yours, are they?

**Caroline** Now, don't you start that.

**Kevin** Why not? (*He picks up the book of love poems*) Is this yours? (*Looking inside*) "To Miss Baxter, with all good . . ." Oh yes, of course. Love poems. I beg your pardon.

**Caroline** (*throwing down her dress and grabbing for the book*) You put that down.

*He holds it away from her*

Give it to me.

**Kevin** No.

**Caroline** (*grabbing hold of it*) Kevin, give it to me.

**Kevin** No.

**Caroline** Let go.

**Kevin** You'll only tear it.

**Caroline** Then let go.

**Kevin** No.

**Caroline** Kevin!

*The book rips in half and falls at their feet*

(*In a white fury*) You bastard . . .! (*She flies at him and claws his face*)

**Kevin** Ow! (*He clutches his face, then grabs hold of Caroline more to protect himself than as a counter-attack*)

**Caroline** (*threshing and flailing*) How dare you destroy my things? How dare you?

**Kevin** (*carrying her bodily to the sofa, trying to calm her*) Caroline, come on, Caroline. Come on or I'll get angry.

**Caroline** You'll get angry? What the hell right have you got to get angry? You're nothing.

**Kevin** (*plonking her on the sofa and pinning her down*) Now, Caroline, pull yourself together, you're——

*Caroline bites him and starts screaming*

Ow! (*He pulls his hand away sharply, hitting her in the face*)

**Caroline** (*stopping her screaming abruptly*) Ah. (*She clutches her eye*)

**Kevin** Sorry, love, I'm sorry. Did I . . .?

**Caroline** Oooh. Ah. Oooh.

**Kevin** You all right?

**Caroline** Yes, I—it's just painful—hang on, ooh.

**Kevin** (*feeling his face*) God, I'm bleeding. You've drawn blood.

**Caroline** I'll just go and bathe it. (*She gets up and sways*) Ooh.

**Kevin** Cold water.

**Caroline** Ow-yow. (*She starts towards the bathroom*)

*The doorbell rings*

Oh, no.

**Kevin** I'll go, I'll go.

*Kevin goes off to the front door*

**Caroline** Ooh-wow-wow . . .

*Caroline goes off to the bathroom*

*Kevin returns, followed by Linda. She is now out of school uniform and looking mature and made up. She carries an envelope. Kevin clutches his face still*

**Kevin** You wanted to see Mrs Hughes?

**Linda** Yes, please.

**Kevin** In what connection?

**Linda** It's just about my tuition. I'm Linda Lawson.

**Kevin** Oh, you're Linda, of course. We met.

**Linda** Yes.

**Kevin** Sorry, I didn't recognize you. You're looking different.

**Linda** Yes, well. I'm going out.

**Kevin** Yes.

*They stare at each other*

Well, I'll go and get Mrs Hughes.

**Linda** Yes. (*She stares at the torn book on the ground. Then at Caroline's dress thrown down*)

**Kevin** (*noticing her look*) Ah. (*He picks up the dress and puts it on a chair, then the book*) Fell apart.

*Caroline re-enters from the bathroom, clasping a flannel to her eye*

**Caroline** Oh, Linda.

**Linda** Mrs Hughes.

**Caroline** What can I—what can I do for you?

**Linda** I just brought round what I owed you, Mrs Hughes. For my classes. (*She holds out the envelope*)

**Caroline** Oh, but you needn't have come round now. On a Saturday. I mean, next time would have done.

**Linda** No, I shan't be doing any more extra tuition, Mrs Hughes.

**Caroline** You won't?

**Linda** No. It's a bit too expensive.

**Caroline** Really? Well, I'm sure I can reduce it if necessary.

**Linda** No, thank you.
**Caroline** It seems such a shame. I mean, you were getting on so——
**Linda** No, thank you.
**Caroline** Oh. Right. (*She takes the envelope*) Thank you.
**Linda** Good-night, Mrs Hughes. Good-night, Mr Hughes.
**Kevin** Good-night, Linda.
**Caroline** Night.

*Kevin goes to show her out*

**Linda** It's all right, I can find my way.

*Linda goes out*

**Caroline** Oh dear.
**Kevin** I didn't recognize her.
**Caroline** You never do.
**Kevin** Have we got anything I can put on my face?
**Caroline** There's some cream in the cabinet.

*The music for "Two Can Play" starts*

**Kevin** (*as he goes*) How's the eye?
**Caroline** Very sore.
**Kevin** I must shave as well.

*Kevin goes to the bathroom area*

**Caroline** (*as her eye twinges*) Ow-wow. (*She picks up her dress and examines it*)

*The Lights come up on a second area in the bathroom. Kevin is examining his scratched face in the mirror*

**Kevin** Aaaah!

*Caroline puts her dress on the sofa. She opens her handbag and takes out a mirror. She removes the flannel from her eye for the first time. She has a fine black eye coming on*

**Caroline** (*seeing herself in the mirror*) Oh, my God.
**Kevin** (*examining his face*) Oh, hell.
**Caroline** You bastard . . .
**Kevin** You . . .
**Caroline** You . . .
**Kevin** You . . .

## No. 13.  Two Can Play

**Caroline** (*singing*) There are games
Two can play better than one . . .
Starting now
We've seen the end of the fun.
As from tonight
This is a fight.

**Kevin** (*singing as he starts to shave*) I can match
                    Any gambit you choose.
                    On your guard
                    Let's begin.
                    Just be warned
                    That I don't play to lose
                    Never quit
                    Till I win.

**Caroline** (*applying make-up gingerly to her eye*)
                    I throw back the gauntlet in your face
                    Name your weapon, choose your time
                            and place . . .

**Kevin**           You've not picked a mate
                    First to conquer, then castrate.
                    He's wise to you.

**Caroline**        Don't unzip your flies
                    Expecting me to eulogize
                    The party's through.

**Kevin**           I can play
                    Intimate games of intrigue.
                    Little girl,
                    I'm in a different league.
                    On with the farce
                    Now shift your arse.

**Caroline** (*putting on her dress*) I can score
                    I've the world at my feet
                    Open goal—open bed.
                    I'll invite passers-by from the street.
                    Seen the light
                    And it's red
                    You will find a woman seldom can
                    Just lie down and take it like a man.

**Kevin**           You taught
                    I have learned.

**Caroline**        There'll be no man left unturned
                    Have no fear.

**Kevin**           I've had
                    Loaded hints
                    Cut moquette
                    And faded chintz
                    Up to here . . .

**Both**            Here come
                    Just two more
                    Victims of the marriage war
                    Me and you.
                    Life won't be the same
                    Now that we have learnt this game
                    Played by two.

> Two can play
> Love is a dirty, deceitful and
>       dangerous game.

*At the end of the song, both are dressed and ready to go. Kevin has settled for
covering up his scratches with sticking plaster. Caroline wears dark glasses*

*Kevin rejoins Caroline in the sitting-room*

**Kevin** Ready to go, darling?
**Caroline** Ready when you are, darling.

*Kevin and Caroline exit*

### No. 14.   Scene Change

*It is now Ivor and Jilly's dining-room. Present time: evening*

*The table is laid for six in splendid fashion*

*Ivor hurries on in his apron to adjust the table*

*From off, in the other direction, laughter is heard from the sitting-room*

*Jilly comes on, a drink in her hand*

**Ivor** Look at the time.
**Jilly** Yes, all right.
**Ivor** Look at the time.
**Jilly** Don't get hysterical. Simmer down.
**Ivor** But where is she?
**Jilly** She's coming, Bundle.
**Ivor** Is she coming? Have you phoned her?
**Jilly** Yes, I phoned her. She's on the hook again and definitely coming.
   You must make allowances. It's her first outing——
**Ivor** On her own.
**Jilly** Out on her own. You must make allowances.
**Ivor** I am quite prepared to make allowances. I am. Unfortunately the
   boeuf en croûte is not.

*He goes back to the kitchen*

**Jilly** I'll bring them to table then, darling. I'll bring them in.
**Ivor** (*off*) Please. Please.
**Jilly** (*going to the other doorway and calling*) Would you like to come
   through now, everyone. It's all ready. This way.

*Joanna enters first. This is the older version Joanna. She is plumper, more
matronly and a lot of her initial garish impact has been toned down*

*Naylor enters with Matthew. Naylor is a man in his forties. Matthew is
younger, in middle to late thirties*

| | |
|---|---|
| **Joanna** Where's Caroline? Isn't she coming? | **Naylor** It's got this new roof line and improved extractor vents around the rear three-quarter |
| **Jilly** Yes, she is. She's coming. | |

**Joanna** I haven't seen her for ages.
**Jilly** Would you sit there, Joanna?
And Matthew there, please.
**Matthew** Thank you.

panel. They've been changed, I think to its advantage. It's also got typical front-wheel scrabble, unfortunately, if you accelerate hard out of corners which is a bad fault, admittedly, but on the whole——

**Jilly** Naylor, here please. Could you sit next to your wife? Next to Joanna.

*Ivor returns from the kitchen with a bowl of taramasalata*

**Ivor** Have we got everyone sat down?
**Jilly** Yes, all under control, Bundle. Don't flap.
**Ivor** I'm not flapping, Bubbles, I'm not flapping.

**Naylor** (*carrying on remorselessly*) But then I had a test drive on the Five-o-four which had a tendency to under-steer but its performance compared very favourably with the Renault.

**Matthew** Aren't we——? Sorry, excuse me, Naylor. Aren't we one short?
**Jilly** Yes, Caroline's not here, yet.
**Matthew** Oh no, of course. This is the woman who's . . .
**Jilly** Yes, just.
**Joanna** Sad.
**Matthew** Yes.
**Naylor** Is this the girl who's just broken up her marriage?
**Jilly** Yes.
**Joanna** From Kevin Hughes. Such a shame. You remember Kevin, Naylor?
**Naylor** What, that little poof actor? Was she married to him? I'm not surprised.
**Joanna** He wasn't a poof.
**Naylor** He wasn't?
**Joanna** No, take it from me.
**Naylor** Well, you surprise me. I thought this girl only went out with poofs before she married me. Eh, Jilly, eh?

*Jilly smiles*

It's just Ivor we've got to worry about, eh, Ivor?
**Ivor** Now this is taramasalata.
**Joanna** Oh, gorgeous.
**Naylor** Tara-what?
**Matthew** Oh, how delicious.
**Naylor** Sounds like a Spanish poof. (*He laughs*)
**Ivor** It's nothing too exciting but there's all sorts of bits and pieces there to dip in. (*He indicates the raw vegetable cruditées*) So please help yourselves.
**Jilly** Ivor's avocados let him down.
**Matthew** Oh dear.
**Joanna** Shame.

**Naylor** Ivor's what? I thought she said something else for a minute, Ivor. (*He laughs*)

**Jilly** Listen, everyone. When Caroline's here, I think we'd better keep the conversation off Kevin. She's still rather sensitive. Isn't she, Ivor?

**Ivor** Vulnerable. (*He proffers a bowl to Joanna*) Joanna?

**Matthew** This looks delicious.

**Joanna** Thank you.

*The doorbell rings*

**Jilly** Doorbell.

**Ivor** That'll be her. I'll go. Please now, get started, everyone.

*Ivor goes out*

**Joanna** It's a bit unfortunate really that I'm here. I mean, if Caroline's trying to forget Kevin. I think she always thought I was after him anyway.

**Jilly** Well, you were.

**Joanna** Not at all.

**Jilly** Remember that dinner party we had here when she went and——

**Joanna** Don't. Don't remind me of that. I still haven't forgiven her.

**Naylor** What are all these intimate confessions eh, Matt?

**Matthew** I don't know.

**Jilly** They're nothing. Ancient history.

**Joanna** Anyway, we mustn't go on. We'll spoil the image for Matthew.

**Matthew** How do you mean?

**Jilly** Now, Jo——

**Naylor** Coincidence, you know. Me making this film with Jilly. And her knowing Joanna.

**Joanna** Jilly knows everybody—absolutely everybody.

*Ivor returns*

**Ivor** She's just coming.

**Joanna** (*waspishly to Matthew*) Take a first look at your blind date, can't you?

**Matthew** I beg your pardon?

**Jilly** Joanna.

**Joanna** Sorry.

**Matthew** I'm sorry, what was this?

*Caroline enters. She is, it will be noted, due to the time sequence, now wearing a different dress from the last scene and is no longer bruised. She is, though, extremely nervous*

**Jilly** Caroline. (*She rises*)

**Caroline** Hallo.

**Ivor** Here she is. (*He rises*)

**Joanna** Hallo, Caroline. Lovely to see you.

**Jilly** Caroline, now come round and sit over here next to Matthew.

**Matthew** (*also rising*) Hallo.

**Jilly** Goodness, you're frozen. Now this is Matthew. Dr Matthew Drayton. And Joanna you know.
**Caroline** Yes.
**Jilly** And this is Naylor Page all the way from Australia, who's the biggest thing there is in fork lift trucks. And I'm making the film.
**Naylor** And she's making the film. Hallo, happy to meet you, Caroline.
**Jilly** I'm afraid we've all started. Ivor was in a bit of a flap.
**Ivor** I'm not in a flap.
**Jilly** Beg your pardon.
**Ivor** Well, don't keep saying I'm in a flap. (*Proffering a bowl to Caroline*) Caroline?
**Caroline** (*taking something*) Oh, thank you.
**Ivor** I'm not in a flap.
**Jilly** Well. All met.
**Joanna** Yes.
**Matthew** Yes.
**Naylor** This tastes better than it looks.
**Joanna** How are you, Caroline? How's the single life again?

*The music for "Table Talk—Part One" starts*

**Caroline** Extremely well, thank you, Joanna. And how's the double life?
**Joanna** Super. You're looking wonderfully taut and trim. Practically sinewy.
**Caroline** Yes, you've filled out nicely . . . .
**Jilly** (*indicating to Matthew that he should pass something to Caroline*) Matthew, would you . . .
**Matthew** Oh yes, of course. Sorry. (*He proffers a bowl to Caroline*)
**Caroline** (*smiling at him*) Thank you.

*Matthew smiles back*

### No. 15.   Table Talk—Part One

| | |
|---|---|
| **Jilly** | Did you know Roger thing? |
| **Joanna** | Rather tall? Slightly queer? |
| **Jilly** | No, not a bit. |
| **Joanna** | Isn't he? My God. |
| **Jilly** | Moreover |
| | Lenny B told me that—— |
| **Joanna** | Does he still live with Jean? |
| **Jilly** | Not any more. He's with Madge. |
| **Joanna** | My God. |
| **Jilly** | Since April. |
| **Joanna** | Where is Jean? |
| **Naylor** (*to Ivor*) | Driving here |
| **Jilly** | Somewhere in Mexico. |
| **Naylor** | . . . on the M Four. |
| **Joanna** | Still on the booze? |
| **Naylor** | And there was a five mile queue. |

| | | |
|---|---|---|
| **Jilly** | | No, she's drying out. |
| **Ivor** | *(together)* | (*to Naylor*) Good gracious. |
| **Joanna** | | How frightful. |
| **Matthew** (*to Caroline*) | | Been quite a nice day |
| | | When I woke up I thought that |
| | | it was sure to rain. |
| **Naylor** | | We turned off |
| **Jilly** | | They split up |
| **Naylor** | | On to the A-three-four. |
| **Joanna** | | Who's she with now? |
| **Naylor** | | I cut across |
| **Jilly** | | Living on her own. |
| **Joanna** | | My God. |
| **Naylor** | | From the three-two-nine. |
| **Jilly** | | How awful. |
| **Ivor** | *(together)* | My goodness. |
| **Caroline** | | I thought so too. |
| **Matthew** | | Do you like . . . ? |
| **Naylor** | | Bled the brakes |
| **Caroline** | | What did you most enjoy? |
| **Naylor** | | Double de-clutch |
| **Matthew** | | I'm just the same |
| **Naylor** | | Then I hit a bank of fog . . . |
| **Caroline** | | Have you ever thought . . . ? |
| **Joanna** | (*over this* | Nice meeting tonight. |
| **Jilly** | *last*) | Isn't it fun to talk like this |
| | | about our friends |
| | | Who can't be here? |
| **Ivor** | *(together)* | Oh, really. |
| **Matthew** | | Quite often. |
| **Jilly** (*raising her glass*) | | Ivor is the man to thank for |
| | | all of this. |
| | | This meal is his creation. |
| | | Now I claim the right to give |
| | | the man a kiss |
| | | In lieu of an ovation. |
| **Ivor** (*over the last*) | | I owe it all to her, my Jilly. |

*Jilly blows a kiss to Ivor at the other end of the table. Everyone, except Caroline, toasts Ivor. All speak at once*

**Joanna** (*speaking*) Here's to Ivor. Good health, Ivor.
**Jilly** (*speaking*) Ivor, darling. God bless. Thank you.
**Naylor** (*speaking*) Here's to the cook. Well done, cookie.
**Matthew** (*speaking*) Congratulations, Ivor. Absolutely first rate.

*The dinner party freezes as the Lights change and Caroline sings the next*

| | |
|---|---|
| **Caroline** | Far too late to ask the question |
| | How was I to blame? |

> Am I just a woman who is
>     better off alone?
> Will I ever quite forget him?
> He's the only man I've known.
> Is it time to take a lover?
> Is it wrong or is it right?
> I'm uncertain and unsure
> And so alone at——

*The Lights change back abruptly*

| | |
|---|---|
| **Jilly** | Raised the hem |
| **Naylor** | Drained the sump. |
| **Joanna** (*demonstrating*) | Gathered here |
| **Naylor** | Checked the plugs |
| **Jilly** | Lost seven stone |
| **Ivor** | Jolly good. |
| **Joanna** | My God. |
| **Nayor** | Twin camshaft. |
| **Jilly** | Have you tried . . .? |
| **Naylor** | M.p.g. |
| **Joanna** | Not my style. |
| **Naylor** | R.p.m. |
| **Jilly** | She's forty-two |
| **Naylor** | B.h.p. |
| **Joanna** | My God. |
| **Ivor** | Just fancy |
| **Jilly** | Had it dyed |
| **Naylor** | Bottom gear |
| **Matthew** | Do you live far from here? |
| **Joanna** | Wore them just once—— |
| **Caroline** | No, not too far . . . |
| **Naylor** | Driving with a dud rear light. |
| **Jilly** | I can wear a ten |
| **Ivor** ⎱ (*together*) | ⎰ Don't blame you. |
| **Joanna** ⎰ | ⎱ You could do |
| **Jilly** | I was told |
| **Naylor** | VAT |
| **Joanna** | Had they had too much to drink? |
| **Naylor** | Steers to the left |
| **Jilly** | She found them both |
| **Naylor** | Driving with a bald rear tyre. |
| **Joanna** | What did Ronnie say? |
| **Matthew** (*under this last to Caroline*) | I'm quite on my own. We have agreed, my wife and I, to live apart. |
| **Caroline** ⎱ | ⎰ Yes. So have we. |
| **Ivor** ⎰ (*together*) | ⎱ Amazing. |
| **Jilly** ⎰ | ⎱ I swear it. |

| Matthew | Don't you find, now and then |
| Caroline | It's been the same for me—— |
| Matthew | May be at first |
| Caroline | —like going mad |
| Matthew | I admit I feel at times |
| Caroline | Then again I get |

| Matthew ⎫<br>Caroline ⎬ | So lonely |
| Jilly | |
| Joanna *(under this last)* | Nice meeting tonight.<br>Isn't it fun to talk about the<br>  things you like |
| Ivor<br>Naylor | To talk about? |

| Ivor *(raising his glass)* | Jilly is a woman special<br>  and unique<br>I totally adore her.<br>See her as a goddess, see her<br>  as a freak<br>But better not ignore her . . . |
| Jilly *(under this last)* | I leave it all to him, my Ivor. |

*Again, everyone except Caroline drinks a toast to Jilly over the next music section. All speak at once*

**Joanna** *(speaking)* Here's to Jilly. Good health.
**Naylor** *(speaking)* All the best, Jilly. Here's to the film.
**Matthew** *(speaking)* Good health, Jilly. Thank you.
**Ivor** *(speaking)* To Jilly. A toast to Jilly.

*Dinner party again freezes during the next as the Lights change*

| Caroline | Here it comes that age-old question<br>How far can this go?<br>Is it yes, please, if he asks me<br>  or a tactful no? |

*The Lights change abruptly*

| All | Nice feelings tonight<br>Isn't it good to feel the way<br>  you never felt<br>You'd feel again? |

*The song ends. Ivor rises. Matthew and Caroline stay looking at each other*

**Ivor** I'm sorry to rush you, everyone, but I must just go and rescue the second course.
**Jilly** Yes, we'll help you, Ivor. You go and rescue it. *(She rises)*
**Joanna** *(also rising)* Yes, we'll help.
**Ivor** Oh, thank you so much.

*Ivor hurries to the kitchen*

*Jilly and Joanna gather up the dishes*

**Jilly** He's in a flap about his en croûte.
**Joanna** Oh God.
**Naylor** He's in a fair bit of trouble, isn't he? What with that and his avocados. The man obviously needs an overhaul.
**Jilly** (*smiling*) Yes.
**Naylor** Eh, Jo? Needs an overhaul, eh?
**Joanna** Yes, don't keep on, Naylor. There's a love.

*Jilly and Joanna go out with the dishes*

*Naylor sits at the table for a moment. He becomes aware of Caroline and Matthew and feels rather spare*

**Naylor** Well, I'll—er—I'll . . . I'll take something out. (*He picks up a bowl and starts to go*)

*The music for "Table Talk—Part One (Reprise)" begins*

(*As he goes*) I don't know what's going on in there.

*Naylor exits*

### No. 16.  Table Talk—Part One (Reprise)

**Caroline** ⎫    Nice feelings tonight.
**Matthew** ⎬    Isn't it good to feel the way you never felt
⎭    You'd feel again?

*As they look at each other, the Lights fade to Black-out*

# ACT II

## No. 17.  Overture

*Ivor and Jilly's dining-room. Past time: a summer evening*

*The table is set similar to before for six and the room is lit by evening light*

*Ivor hurries on in his apron to adjust the table as the music finishes. From off, in the other direction there is laughter from the sitting-room*

*Jilly comes on, drink in hand*

**Ivor**  Where are they?

**Jilly**  They're coming.

**Ivor**  They are coming, I take it?

**Jilly**  They're coming, Bundle.

**Ivor**  That bloody Kevin is never on time for anything. Why do you have to keep on inviting actors to dinner?

**Jilly**  Now, Ivor . . .

**Ivor**  Urban guerillas. International hijackers. At least they're punctual. Anyone but actors. Train robbers . . .

**Jilly**  Ivor, you really mustn't flap like this.

**Ivor**  That chicken is about to disintegrate. Poulet l'estragon is about to become chicken broth.

**Jilly**  That's lovely, chicken broth, lovely.

**Ivor**  Not for a main course and not when we're having soup to start with.

**Jilly**  Tonight? It's sweltering. Do we want soup?

**Ivor**  Watercress. Cold watercress soup.

**Jilly**  That'll be nice. That can't get cold, anyway, can it?

**Ivor**  It can get warm. I took it out of the fridge to make room for the bavarois á l'orange.

*He goes back into the kitchen*

**Jilly**  I'll bring everyone to the table then, darling, shall I?

**Ivor**  (*off*) Yes, please. Do please.

**Jilly**  (*going to the other doorway and calling*) Would you all like to come through now, folks? It's on the table. Come and get it.

*Joanna enters first. Her younger, slimmer self*

**Joanna**  They've arrived. Caroline and Kevin. They've arrived.

**Jilly**  Oh, thank heavens. Ivor was getting unbearable.

*Howard enters. He is a genial if ineffectual man in his mid-thirties, rather overweight*

**Joanna** God knows what they've been up to. Those two.

**Jilly** How do you mean?

**Joanna** Wait till you see them.

**Howard** Now then, what's Ivor cooking up for us tonight?

**Jilly** Apparently, poulet l'estragon.

**Howard** (*quite excited*) Ah-ha.

**Jilly** Come and sit here, Howard. And I've put you here next to him, Joanna.

**Joanna** Fine.

**Howard** Poulet l'estragon. Now that's interesting. I went with a chum nearly to Dulwich—I should say, all but Dulwich—for a poulet l'estragon. Certainly we got within a whisker of Dulwich . . .

**Jilly** That sounds an awful long way to go just for roast chicken, doesn't it, Howard?

**Howard** My God, Jilly, I'm talking about poulet l'estragon. Not roast chicken. I wouldn't cross the road for a chicken.

**Joanna** (*laughing*) Ha ha. That's very funny.

**Jilly** (*seeing the joke*) Oh yes. (*She joins Joanna in laughing*)

**Howard** (*slightly puzzled*) Yes . . . (*He laughs half-heartedly with them*)

*They finish laughing*

What are we laughing at?

**Joanna** (*exasperated*) My God.

*Ivor enters with the soup*

**Ivor** Here we are.

**Howard** Ah-ha. Ah-ha. (*Rubbing his hands together*) Looks like soup.

**Ivor** Soup it is. (*To Jilly*) Bubbles, are they coming?

**Jilly** Yes, Bundle, they're coming. They're coming.

**Howard** I say, this looks good. (*He is looking into the soup tureen*)

**Ivor** Well, where are they?

**Howard** Cucumber?

**Ivor** Watercress.

**Howard** Watercress, eh? First rate. First rate.

*Kevin and Caroline enter together. He with the sticking plaster on his scratched face; she in dark glasses*

**Jilly** (*rising to greet them*) There they are now. Heavens, what's happened to you both?

**Kevin** Hallo. Sorry we're late. We had a little accident.

**Ivor** In the taxi?

**Caroline** On foot.

**Kevin** Before we left.

**Jilly** Are you both all right?

**Caroline** It was so stupid. I was running through the door with my hand out, like this, and Kevin was behind it and he ran into me—like this . . . (*She demonstrates*) Like that, you see.

*The others, including Kevin, study this unconvincing reconstruction*

**Jilly** How dreadful.
**Joanna** Awful.
**Ivor** Dear dear.
**Howard** Why were you running like that?
**Caroline** Like what?
**Howard** With your arms sticking out.
**Caroline** Oh, well—I do that quite a bit. That's how I run.
**Howard** Really.
**Joanna** And this is when you hurt your eye? Was Kevin running about in the same way?
**Caroline** Er, no—he——
**Kevin** No. I punched her . . .
**Joanna** Oh.
**Kevin** In the eye.
**Ivor** Ah.
**Howard** Oh.
**Jilly** ⎫
            ⎬ *(together)* ⎰ Well, come and sit down. I've put you both round here.
**Ivor**  ⎭            ⎱ *(Indicating chairs)* Caroline. Kevin.
                        Yes, well, would you like to help yourself, Joanna?
                        *(He proffers the tureen)*
**Joanna** Thank you.
**Caroline** So sorry we're late, Ivor.
**Jilly** Now, you haven't met Howard, have you? Howard Potter, this is Caroline and Kevin Hughes.
**Caroline** Hallo.
**Howard** How do you do.
**Kevin** Hallo.
**Jilly** Howard is in soft furnishings.
**Kevin** Oh, that's interesting.
**Howard** Fairly, yes.
**Jilly** Are you going to wear your glasses all through dinner, Caroline?
**Caroline** Sorry, if you don't mind.
**Ivor** Awfully sinister. *(Offering her the soup)* Caroline?
**Caroline** Thank you.
**Joanna** I think it makes her look very mysterious and extremely interesting. Great improvement. *(She laughs)*
**Caroline** Glad you think so.
**Howard** This looks awfully good, you know, Ivor.
**Jilly** It's a terribly warm evening, isn't it?
**Joanna** Dreadful.
**Kevin** You look cool enough.
**Joanna** Oh, I'm always pretty cool.
**Kevin** Really?
**Howard** Do you use garlic?
**Ivor** Yes, yes. Just a little.
**Jilly** We'd've eaten outdoors only we'd have been bitten to death.

**Howard** Egg yolks?

*The music for "Table Talk—Part Two" starts*

**Ivor** Yes.
**Joanna** You've got a tan.
**Kevin** Just from the garden.
**Howard** Cream?
**Ivor** Yes.

*Caroline thrusts the soup tureen at Kevin*

**Kevin** Thank you, dearest.
**Howard** Olive oil?
**Ivor** Yes.
**Howard** I know the one. Delicious. Do you use spring onions?
**Ivor** No, just the normal.
**Howard** Try it with spring onions. It adds a little . . .

### No. 18.  Table Talk—Part Two

| | |
|---|---|
| **Jilly** | I have heard |
| | Jenny J—— |
| **Joanna** | —left her job . . . |
| **Kevin** | I heard that . . . |
| **Jilly** | Right round the bend |
| **Caroline** | Who is this? |
| **Joanna** | My God. |
| **Jilly** | So Bill said. |
| **Kevin** | I heard that |
| | Second hand . . . |
| **Joanna** | She was calm. Very sane. |
| **Jilly** | Not any more. |
| **Kevin** | Flipped her lid. |
| **Joanna** | My God. |
| **Caroline** | Who's Jenny? |
| **Kevin** | How is she? |
| **Howard** (*to Ivor*) | We were out |
| **Jilly** | I haven't heard a word |
| **Howard** | At this new place |
| **Joanna** | Where is she now? |
| **Howard** | And we had a damn good meal |
| **Jilly** | She won't see a soul |
| **Ivor** } (*together*) | { (*to Howard*) Where's this then? |
| **Caroline** } | { Who's Jenny? |
| **Howard** | Dover sole |
| **Joanna** | She was so |
| **Jilly** | Nobody's seen her since |
| **Howard** | Served off the bone |
| **Jilly** | Without a trace |

| | |
|---|---|
| **Howard** | Mushrooms à la grêcque |
| **Caroline** | Oh dear . . . |
| **Howard** | And crêpe suzette. |
| **Kevin** (*under this last*) | Don't think that we've met |
| | Since we were both together |
| | doing Sanilene. |

| | | |
|---|---|---|
| **Joanna** | | Don't mention that. |
| **Caroline** | (*together*) | How dreadful . . . |
| **Ivor** | | Where's this then? |

| | |
|---|---|
| **Jilly** | Have you read . . .? |
| **Howard** | Then we had . . . |
| **Jilly** | If you should get the chance . . . |
| **Howard** | Château Latour |
| **Jilly** | Right up your street |
| **Howard** | In a really perfect sauce. |
| **Jilly** | Couldn't put it down. |

| | | |
|---|---|---|
| **Kevin** | (*over this* | Nice meeting like this |
| **Joanna** | *last*) | Isn't it fun to talk about the |
| | | jobs you wish |
| | | You'd never done? |

| | | |
|---|---|---|
| **Ivor** | (*together*) | Sounds lovely. |
| **Caroline** | | I'll try to. |

| | |
|---|---|
| **Jilly** | Ivor is the one responsible for this |
| | It's all his inspiration. |
| | No-one's going to mind me |
| | giving him a kiss |
| | As my appreciation. |
| **Ivor** (*under this last*) | I owe it all to her, my Jilly. |

*Jilly blows kiss to Ivor at the other end of the table. Everyone except Caroline, toasts Ivor. All speak at once*

**Howard** (*speaking*) Here's to a first rate soup. One of the best I've tasted.
**Jilly** (*speaking*) Congratulations, darling, as always.
**Joanna** (*speaking*) Here's to Ivor. Good health, Ivor.
**Kevin** (*speaking*) A toast to Ivor. All the best, mate.

*The dinner party freezes as the Lights change and Caroline, who has been registering Kevin and Joanna's increasingly friendly tête à tête, sings the next*

| | |
|---|---|
| **Caroline** | Someone kindly ask my husband |
| | Does he know I'm here? |
| | Maybe he's forgotten I'm the |
| | the woman that he brought. |
| | Does he think that I'm short-sighted |
| | With a mean IQ of nought? |
| | Should I start to scream my head off? |
| | Or just smile and be polite? |
| | Should we both call it a day |
| | And sleep alone at—— |

*The Lights change back abruptly*

| | | |
|---|---|---|
| **Jilly** | | Black and white |
| **Howard** | | Salmon mousse |
| **Joanna** | | Turned me down |
| **Howard** | | Cordon Bleu |
| **Kevin** | | They must be mad |
| **Ivor** | | Rather rich |
| **Joanna** (*shrilly*) | | Ha! Ha! |
| **Howard** | | In aspic. |
| **Jilly** | | Those old films |
| **Kevin** | | You look more—— |
| **Howard** | | In white wine. |
| **Joanna** | | Do you think? |
| **Kevin** | | Each time we meet. |
| **Jilly** | | Knew their job. |
| **Joanna** | | Oh—you . . . |
| **Ivor** | | Fantastic. |
| **Howard** | | À la carte. |
| **Kevin** | | You were great . . . |
| **Jilly** | | Think of the gear they had . . . |
| **Joanna** | | Did you think that? |
| **Howard** | | In olive oil. |
| **Kevin** | | Everybody thought you great. |
| **Jilly** | | . . . time that they were made . . . |
| **Ivor** | (*together*) | Where *is* this? |
| **Joanna** | | Well, thank you. |
| **Howard** | | Melba toast. |
| **Kevin** | | You are rare. |
| **Joanna** | | Thought I was good in that. |
| **Howard** | | Masses of cream. |
| **Kevin** | | You've got the shape |
| **Jilly** | | Coupled it with Schubert's "Trout". |
| **Howard** | | In a silver dish. |
| **Ivor** | (*together*) | Unusual. |
| **Joanna** | | (*laughing*) You're joking. |
| **Caroline** | (*under this last*) | She's driving me mad—— |
| | | Doing my best to keep control |
| | | but very soon |
| | | I'm going to throw—— |
| **Kevin** | | In my view, you could play—— |
| **Joanna** | | I would be good in that. |
| **Kevin** | | Someone like you |
| **Joanna** | | I need the chance |
| **Kevin** | | You won't have to wait long |
| **Joanna** | | Darling, you and I |
| **Kevin** | | |
| **Joanna** | | We'll make it. |

| | |
|---|---|
| **Jilly** ⎤ | Nice meeting tonight. |
| **Caroline** ⎟ | Isn't it fun to talk about the |
| **Howard** ⎬ | things you like |
| **Ivor** ⎦ | To talk about? |
| **Ivor** | Jilly has a mind that's capable |
| | and strong |
| | You never can predict her. |
| | Praise her if she's right but if |
| | she's ever wrong |
| | Don't try to contradict her . . . |
| **Jilly** (*under this last*) | I let him run my life, my Ivor . . . |

*Again, everyone except Caroline, drinks a toast to Jilly over the next music section. All speak at once*

**Joanna** (*speaking*) Here's to Jilly. A toast to Jilly.
**Howard** (*speaking*) Here's to our hostess. Very good health.
**Ivor** (*speaking*) To Jilly. The one and only.
**Kevin** (*speaking*) All the best, Jilly.

*Dinner party again freezes during the next as the Lights change and Caroline sings*

| | |
|---|---|
| **Caroline** | Here am I, till now behaving |
| | Rather like a saint. |
| | Witness now this self-same woman |
| | Losing her restraint. |

*The Lights change back*

| | |
|---|---|
| **All** | Nice feelings tonight. |
| | Isn't it good to feel the way |
| | you never felt |
| | You'd feel again? |

*The song ends. Ivor rises. Kevin and Joanna stay looking at each other*

**Ivor** Excuse me everyone, I must dash. Things are a bit critical in the kitchen, excuse me.

*Ivor goes out*

**Jilly** (*also rising*) Oh dear, perhaps I ought to give him a hand.
**Caroline** (*getting up abruptly*) No, let me. Let's all carry something shall we?

*Caroline snatches up hers and Kevin's soup bowls and goes out*

**Howard** Well, let me . . . (*He rises*)
**Jilly** (*gathering up her and Ivor's bowls*) No, sit there, we'll . . .
**Howard** (*gathering up his and Joanna's bowls*) No, no. It's a good excuse to see Ivor in action at the nerve centre. I want to know if he uses madeira or port in his sauce.
**Jilly** I hope he's using cooking sherry.
**Howard** Hardly, hardly.

*Howard goes out*

**Jilly** (*following him*) Don't crowd him, Howard. If you get too near, he lashes out.

*Jilly goes off after Howard*

*Joanna and Kevin are alone. They sing*

### No. 19.   Table Talk—Part Two (Reprise)

**Joanna**  }
**Kevin**  }                    Nice feelings tonight

*Caroline enters. She goes and collects the soup tureen. Joanna and Kevin do not notice her*

> Isn't it good to feel the way you never felt
> You'd feel——

*Caroline, passing behind Joanna, rather deliberately ladles soup down the back of her dress*

**Joanna**  }(*together*)  {(*screaming*) Aaaah!
**Kevin**   }             {What the hell . . .?
**Caroline** Oh, I am sorry.
**Joanna** What are you doing? What are you doing?
**Caroline** Oh dear, I'm sorry.
**Joanna** Did you do that deliberately?
**Kevin** She did it deliberately.
**Caroline** Yes. Yes, I did. You're absolutely right. I'm sorry.
**Joanna** How dare you? It's running down my . . . aaah. (*She wriggles*) You vicious, vindictive, repressed, neurotic little teacher.
**Caroline** (*crouching aggressively and brandishing the tureen and ladle*) Want some more? Want some more?
**Kevin** Caroline!
**Joanna** (*retreating; shrilly*) Get away! Get away!
**Caroline** (*advancing*) More soup? Want some more soup, do you?

*Joanna shrieks*

**Kevin** Caroline. Stop it. Stop it at once.
**Caroline** Soup—soup—soup.

*Jilly enters with plates*

**Jilly** What on earth's going on?
**Joanna** Stop her. Somebody stop her.
**Jilly** Caroline!
**Kevin** Now, come on, darling . . .
**Caroline** Anybody else want seconds?
**Jilly** (*thundering with authority*) Caroline, put that down at once!

*Caroline does so*

> That's better.

**Joanna** Look at my dress. Look at me. (*To Kevin*) Can't you keep your wife under control? She shouldn't be allowed out. She's off her head. (*She starts out*)
**Jilly** Where are you going?
**Joanna** I'm going home.

*Joanna goes out*

**Kevin** (*going off after her*) Oh hell. (*To Caroline*) What did you . . . ? Joanna, Joanna, wait a tick . . . I'll take you home . . .

*Kevin goes off after her*

**Caroline** (*yelling*) That's right. Go and rub watercress into her back.

*A pause. Caroline is aware of Jilly's icy gaze*

(*Very penitently*) I'm sorry.
**Jilly** I should think so too. (*She laughs*) I don't think that was awfully wise, Caroline.
**Caroline** What?
**Jilly** Letting Kev take Joanna home. It's asking for trouble.
**Caroline** That's all right. My husband and I have an arrangement.
**Jilly** You do?
**Caroline** Oh yes. Easy come, easy go—that's us. We believe frankly that that is the only way a marriage can hope to stay fresh. And stimulating. And constantly developing.
**Jilly** Yes, I see. Carry on convincing me.
**Caroline** You see, it's very important, we feel . . . (*She starts to cry as she says the next*) . . . never to take your love for each other for granted. You see. And then if you want . . . if you want . . . (*She has become inaudible*)
**Jilly** (*straining to comprehend*) I'm sorry, darling, what are you saying?
**Caroline** (*little more than a series of squeaks now*) I'm just saying if you want . . . if you want . . . I don't know what I'm saying . . .
**Jilly** You don't know what you're saying.
**Caroline** No.
**Jilly** Caroline.
**Caroline** Ummm?
**Jilly** This isn't the way, is it, dear?
**Caroline** (*shaking her head*) No.
**Jilly** You're going to have to get on top of this.
**Caroline** Mmmm. (*She nods*)
**Jilly** Before you're completely destroyed. Now sit down.
**Caroline** Mmm?
**Jilly** Sit down. Have a glass of wine. (*She pours her one*)

*Caroline sits*

Now then.
**Caroline** I'm sorry I've ruined your dinner party.

**Jilly** It's Ivor you ought to apologize to.

**Caroline** Do you think that Howard man would mind, very quickly, running me over to home. To home. To my home . . .

**Jilly** I don't know. I don't think it really matters whether he minds or not. (*Calling*) Howard, dearest?

*Howard comes in juggling with his hot vegetable dish. He's obviously been waiting by the door*

**Howard** Oh, you've finished, have you? Jolly good. It's very hot, this, very hot. Ivor's keeping the sauce at bay.

**Jilly** Howard . . .

**Howard** (*setting down the dish*) Ah. (*To Jilly*) Jilly?

**Jilly** Would you be an absolute sweetheart and mind running Caroline to home. Rather, home.

**Howard** Not at all. My pleasure. When you both want to leave, just give me a yell. Only too pleased. Excuse me, I'll just get the potatoes. (*He moves to the door*)

**Jilly** Howard?

**Howard** Uh?

**Jilly** I think Caroline is giving you a yell now.

**Howard** I beg your pardon?

**Jilly** She wants to go to home now.

**Caroline** To home.

**Howard** Now? But we're just getting to the main course. Aren't you staying for the main course? (*To Jilly*) Isn't she staying for the main course?

**Caroline** It wouldn't take a second. We're not that far.

**Howard** Are you ill? (*To Jilly*) Is she ill?

**Jilly** She just wants to go home, Howard.

**Howard** Well, can't your husband—can't her husband take her?

**Jilly** Howard, you're being awfully ungallant.

**Howard** But I'm going to miss my meal, aren't I?

**Jilly** Kevin has already gone.

**Howard** He's gone too?

**Jilly** Yes.

**Howard** After the soup?

**Jilly** He's taken Joanna to home.

**Howard** Joanna?

**Caroline** In lieu of a main course.

**Howard** I don't follow any of this. Let's get this straight. Who's actually staying on for the main course?

**Jilly** Nobody.

**Howard** Why has Joanna left? I thought she was with me.

**Jilly** She didn't care for the soup.

**Howard** What?

**Jilly** Look, Howard, give Caroline a quick lift home and then come straight back, there's an angel.

**Howard** (*reluctantly*) All right. You'll leave some for me, will you?

**Jilly** Howard, you've seen what he's doing in there. He's cooked enough
for fourteen.

**Howard** All right, all right. (*To Caroline*) Are you ready?

**Caroline** Thank you very much. It's not far. It's only a crow's throw. As
the stone flies . . .

**Howard** I'll reverse out then. This is a most extraordinary evening.

*Howard goes out*

**Caroline** Good-night, Jilly.

**Jilly** Good-night. Caroline . . .

**Caroline** Yes?

**Jilly** Don't do anything you'll regret in the morning, will you?

**Caroline** Wait and see.

*Caroline goes*

### No. 20.   Caroline's Exit

*Jilly begins to tidy the table, clearing the places, so it is now laid for three*

*Ivor enters with an enormous steaming serving dish*

**Ivor** I'm sorry about this, everyone. I had a little bit of trouble mixing up
the . . . Where have they gone?

**Jilly** Hallo, Ivor. I'm so glad you could join me.

**Ivor** Eh?

*The music peaks. The Lights cross fade*

*Ivor and Jilly exit*

*We move from the dining-room to Caroline's flat. It is present time*

*There is the sound of the flat door being opened*

*Matthew and Caroline come in as the music stops*

**Caroline** (*as she enters*) Brr. It's freezing. (*She turns on the lights*)

**Matthew** (*entering behind her*) Yes, it's pretty cold.

**Caroline** Now, when I say coffee, I actually mean instant, I'm afraid.

**Matthew** Well, this time of night . . .

**Caroline** (*indicating the flat*) Sorry about the mess.

**Matthew** Oh yes. Late spring cleaning, are you?

**Caroline** No, no. I don't believe in that. Never clean. Happy-go-lucky,
that's me.

**Matthew** Really?

**Caroline** (*removing her coat*) Where it falls, let it lie. (*She throws her coat
casually on to the floor*) Hang on, I'll put the kettle on. If I can find it.
(*She laughs*)

*Caroline goes into the kitchen, switching on the record player as she passes*

## No. 21.   Record Player Music

*Matthew looks doubtfully at her coat. He takes off his own, deliberates for a second on whether to throw his on the floor, decides against it, picks hers up and lays both coats neatly on the end of the sofa. He moves some other bric à brac and sits*

*Caroline returns*

Won't be a sec. No, you see, I decided that when my husband walked out, I was going to turn over a new leaf. (*She sits*)

**Matthew** Oh yes.

**Caroline** No more being boringly houseproud. All that furniture polishing and mopping and scrubbing and wiping and shining. Do you know, I got to the state I used to clean my self-cleaning oven once a week because I didn't trust it. When I wasn't cleaning this flat, I was cleaning my cleaning materials.

**Matthew** Were you?

**Caroline** I was obsessional. My husband was right. He was right and he left.

**Matthew** You're divorced?

**Caroline** No.

**Matthew** Ah.

**Caroline** Are you?

**Matthew** Not yet. My wife is—in the process.

**Caroline** I see. Process of what?

**Matthew** Of starting proceedings.

**Caroline** I see.

**Matthew** I'm having to be a little cautious as a result. I'm contesting it, you see. I'm contesting her grounds.

**Caroline** What are they?

**Matthew** Cruelty.

**Caroline** Oh. (*Tentatively*) Physical?

**Matthew** Good Lord, no.

**Caroline** Oh, mental?

**Matthew** Of course.

**Caroline** Yes, of course. What did you do?

**Matthew** I didn't do anything. It's what she says I did.

**Caroline** What does she say you did?

**Matthew** She claims I—chivvied her.

**Caroline** Chivvied her? What—"come along, darling, pull your finger out"—that sort of thing?

**Matthew** I've no idea.

**Caroline** You must have done something.

**Matthew** Not that I know of. I can't even remember chivvying her.

**Caroline** Extraordinary. Still, what is mental cruelty? We're probably all guilty of it, every day.

**Matthew** I don't think so.

**Caroline** I've been cruel. I've hurt my husband. I've hurt my friends. I've

even hurt my students sometimes. Kids in my class. Just saying things,
the wrong things.

**Matthew** That sounds more like thoughtlessness. Not quite the same
thing.

**Caroline** It still hurts.

**Matthew** True.

**Caroline** Do you know, this weekend, for me it's been a weekend for
seeing things.

**Matthew** What?

**Caroline** The folly of my ways. The light. A woman came to see me
yesterday. A colleague. And I saw myself in her. Eaten up by ob-
sessions. Things that no longer matter, not even to her. Her life had
been stunted. And then today, I saw my father and there he was,
fossilized, still pretending he's carrying on a happy marriage that
finished three years ago.

**Matthew** Perhaps that makes him happy.

**Caroline** I wouldn't mind that. But he keeps holding it up as an example
to the rest of the world. To me. This is how to live happily, girl. Both
of us permanently eighty miles apart. Me here and her in Bournemouth.
No, I have resolved this. From today, my life is going to be lived for
today and only for today. I'm going to stop worrying about little things,
stop bellyaching about minutiae, about chair covers and sheets and
whether you've rolled up your table napkin properly. I'm about to
enjoy every remaining second of my life. I'm . . . Sorry, I'm talking
too much.

**Matthew** No.

**Caroline** Yes, I am.

**Matthew** Not at all.

**Caroline** My God, you're thinking, what have I landed myself with?

**Matthew** No. I was actually thinking that you're rather fascinating.

**Caroline** Were you?

**Matthew** Yes.

**Caroline** Oh. (*An embarrassed pause. She laughs*) Follow that, eh? Makes
a change. People don't often tell me that.

**Matthew** Depends how many people you bring back for coffee.

**Caroline** Oh no, no. I'm very fussy about who dips into my coffee
powder.

**Matthew** I'm honoured.

**Caroline** Not just anyone gets in here, you know. With fascinating people
like me . . .

*The Lights change to past time*

*Howard comes out of the kitchen holding a milk bottle*

**Howard** Want milk in it, do you?

**Caroline** (*drunkenly*) Yes, please.

**Howard** Righto.

*Howard goes back into the kitchen*

*The Lights change back to present time*

**Matthew** I think it's probably boiling by now, isn't it?

**Caroline** (*coming out of her reverie*) What? Oh yes. Hang on. (*She starts to rise*)

**Matthew** No, let me.

**Caroline** It's all right, I'll . . .

**Matthew** Please, let me. Sit down. (*Gently but firmly*) Sit.

**Caroline** (*sitting*) OK. You won't know where everything is.

**Matthew** I'll find it. You take it easy.

*Matthew goes out to the kitchen*

**Caroline** Good heavens . . .

*The Lights change to past time again and are darker*

*Howard enters from the kitchen with a cup of coffee*

**Howard** Here we are. You've only got that instant stuff, did you know?

**Caroline** Yes, that's all we drink.

**Howard** How absolutely appalling. There you are. (*He gives her the cup*)

**Caroline** Thank you.

**Howard** It's very dark in here. Do you want some more light?

**Caroline** No. I prefer the dark.

**Howard** Is that why you were wearing the glasses earlier?

**Caroline** Yes. I'm hideously disfigured. I don't want you to see.

**Howard** Really?

**Caroline** I was lion tamer for some time. There was an accident. Simba went crazy. He ate the chair and then he started on me.

**Howard** Yes, right, well. Good-night, then.

**Caroline** Don't go yet. Aren't you having coffee?

**Howard** Certainly not. I'm only one third of the way through my meal. I have poulet l'estragon and from my quick look in the fridge, what looked like bavarois à l'orange to follow with possibly some Stilton after that. When I do start on my coffee in about an hour, I shall make sure it's freshly ground, infused not percolated and served very hot and very black. Good-night.

**Caroline** Sit down.

**Howard** What?

**Caroline** Sit down. I haven't finished with you.

**Howard** I beg your pardon?

**Caroline** You don't think I asked you in for a chat, do you?

**Howard** No. I think you asked me in because you couldn't have made it up the stairs on your own. (*He laughs*)

**Caroline** Rubbish.

**Howard** Frankly, you're rather drunk. If you don't mind my saying so . . .

**Caroline** Sit down.

**Howard** Look, I'm expected back. (*He sits*) What can I do for you?

**Caroline** Well. My husband's gone off with that—with your—girl friend. So. Fair's fair, eh?

**Howard** No, I don't follow this.

**Caroline** You've lost your woman—so——

**Howard** No, no, no.

**Caroline** What?

**Howard** Not my woman.

**Caroline** You brought her to dinner with you or have you forgotten?

**Howard** Yes. Not my woman, though. I got her from this place.

**Caroline** What place?

**Howard** This agency. This escort agency.

**Caroline** Escort agency?

**Howard** Yes.

**Caroline** You mean you rented her? You rented Joanna?

**Howard** I don't think they call it that in so many words. Escort fee or something.

**Caroline** But why? Why rent her?

**Howard** Well . . .

**Caroline** You must be the only person who's ever had to pay.

**Howard** It's a lot more convenient, really. You phone up. Send me a woman, please. You meet up, take her out somewhere. Give her a meal, bore her stiff with your problems, put her in a taxi and send her home. Much the best way. Difficult eating alone, you know. (*Fumbling in his wallet*) Look, if you're desperate yourself, why don't you try them? They're called Just Good Friends. I think they do men as well as women. Just ring them and they'll whistle one round. They're usually quite reasonable types. Actors mostly.

**Caroline** No, thank you. Not actors.

**Howard** Oh yes, sorry. I forgot, your . . .

**Caroline** Wait till I've finished my coffee. I haven't finished with you yet. I'll tell you about good friends. (*She puts the coffee cup down*)

*The Lights change to present time*

*Matthew returns with two cups of coffee*

**Matthew** Here we are. I had to wash a couple of cups. (*Seeing the cup by Caroline which she has just put down*) Oh, there are more in here.

**Caroline** Sorry. Standards have slipped a little lately.

**Matthew** Well, it's understandable. Sudden change of lifestyle. It affects people in odd ways, doesn't it? When Anne—when my wife left me, I remember—silly—I remember I didn't clean my shoes for weeks.

**Caroline** Good heavens.

**Matthew** Extraordinary, wasn't it?

**Caroline** Yes. Extraordinary to meet a man who cleans his shoes anyway. Mind you, my husband only wore sneakers. They became welded to his feet with age.

**Matthew** Oh dear. No, I think you owe it to the world to clean your shoes occasionally.

**Caroline** Quite right. So you do. Well . . .

**Matthew** Yes.

**Caroline** Here we are.

**Matthew** Yes.

**Caroline** (*raising her coffee cup*) Thank you for this.

**Matthew** My pleasure.

**Howard** Look, if I'm going to be here much longer, I think I'm going to have to make myself a sandwich to tide me over.

*The music for "What Do They Expect" starts*

**Caroline** (*fiercely*) Wait.

*Howard sits unhappily. Caroline smiles at Howard, who smiles back feebly. Matthew smiles at Caroline who smiles back. The men smile at Caroline and Caroline smiles at the men*

## No. 22.  What Do They Expect?

| | |
|---|---|
| **Matthew** | What does she expect of me?<br>What's she hoping the trend will be?<br>Is she saying yes or no?<br>Does she want me to stay or go?<br>How am I meant to interpret<br>All her significant looks?<br>I find this business of chatting up women<br>A bloody sight simpler in books . . . |
| **Caroline** | Somebody,<br>What do they expect of you?<br>I've done everything I can do.<br>Wherefore does he hesitate?<br>Is he wanting it on a plate?<br>Short of removing my clothing<br>Rolling around on the floor<br>Or does he want me to shout come and get it?<br>What's he just sitting there for? |
| **Matthew** ⎫<br>**Caroline** ⎭ | Here we are<br>You and I<br>Playing waiting games<br>Anticipating games<br>Blind man's buff<br>Hide and seek<br>Look at us—you won't guess<br>Deep inside we both are wondering . . . |
| **Caroline** | What does he expect of me?<br>Does he know that it's all for free? |
| **Matthew** | What on earth does she expect?<br>Would that women were more direct . . . |
| **Matthew** ⎫<br>**Caroline** ⎭ | We could be sat here forever<br>Neither one daring to move |
| **Caroline** | Or does he want me to feel unattractive? |

| | |
|---|---|
| **Matthew** | What is she trying to prove? |
| **Matthew**  ⎫<br>**Caroline**  ⎬ | Honestly . . . |
| **Howard** | What does she expect of me?<br>She's presuming telepathy.<br>I have seen her to her door<br>Is she hoping we'll take the floor? |
| **Matthew** | Is it bye-bye or the bedroom? |
| **Caroline** | Is he just rigid with fear? |
| **Howard** | I do so hope she's not wanting athletics. |
| **Caroline** | Maybe he's secretly queer . . . |
| **Caroline**  ⎫<br>**Howard**  ⎬<br>**Matthew**  ⎭ | Here we are<br>You and I<br>Playing mating games<br>Non-procreating games<br>Postman's knock<br>Kiss and tell<br>Look at us. You won't guess<br>Deep inside we all are questioning . . . |

*Kevin and Joanna enter a separate area and the Lights come up on them.*
*They are standing on her doorstep. He holds her soup-stained dress while*
*she, in her borrowed mac, is fumbling in her handbag for her front-door key*

| | |
|---|---|
| **Joanna** | What does he expect of me?<br>Dare I spurn his virility? |
| **Kevin** | Is it likely she'll resist?<br>Notwithstanding she's slightly pissed . . . |
| **Caroline** | He must crack sooner or later |
| **Kevin** | May I come near and how far? |
| **Matthew** | Do we read coffee to mean something greater? |
| **All** | Please let us know where we are.<br>Anyone . . .<br>What do they expect of us?<br>Is there anything to discuss?<br>Are they meaning yes or no?<br>Would it spoil it by saying so . . .? |
| **Caroline** | I've reached the point of frustration |
| **Joanna** | Too many things are unsaid |
| **Howard**  ⎫<br>**Kevin**  ⎬<br>**Matthew**  ⎭ | Do they need friendship or straight fornication? |
| **Caroline** | Either way I need my bed. |
| **All** | Wish I knew<br>What—they—expect. |

*Howard, Joanna and Kevin go as the song finishes*

*We return to present time only. Alone, Caroline and Matthew smile at each*
*other*

## No. 23.   Matthew and Caroline

**Matthew** (*at length*) Well . . . (*He rises, suddenly decisive*) Look, I'm going home now.
**Caroline** Please, don't feel you . . .
**Matthew** I think I'd better. (*He thinks*) Yes. Yes, I think I'd better. Don't see me out. It's all right.

*Caroline half rises*

(*Forcefully*) Please. Don't see me out. Stay just where you are. (*He backs to the door*) I'd just like to say that I would very much like to see you again. If that's all right.
**Caroline** Yes.
**Matthew** Right. I'll ring you, shall I?
**Caroline** Please. Yes, please. Please. Please.
**Matthew** Bye.
**Caroline** Bye.

*After one last lingering glance at her, he goes*

(*Yelling*) Matthew! You haven't got the number! Matthew . . .
**Matthew** (*off, distant*) Two-o-five, five-one-two-two.
**Caroline** (*calling*) Don't forget.

## No. 24.   Montage Sequence

(*She shakes her head in disbelief*) What a simply amazing, incredible, attractive, unbelievably mind-bending man. And he's a doctor.

*The music peaks*

*Caroline exits*

*The Lights fade down and then come up again. The phone rings*

*Caroline comes racing through the front door clutching a bottle of brandy*

*The music finishes*

(*As she enters*) Don't ring off. Please don't ring off. I'm coming, I'm coming . . . (*She answers the phone*) Hallo . . . Oh, thank God. Matt, where are you? . . . Sorry, no. I just popped out to buy you some brandy. . . . I remembered you. . . . Oh, I see. . . . Well, when can you get . . . ? But I've got everything cooking, I've. . . . I've made you. . . . No. . . . No, that's all right. . . . Yes—so do I. . . . Me, you. . . . Yes. . . . 'Bye. (*She rings off. She is suddenly very low*) Oh. Oh, bollocks.

*Anne Drayton, a thin nervous woman, about the same age as Caroline, is in the doorway behind her*

**Anne** Mrs Hughes?
**Caroline** (*wheeling round*) Oh Lord, who are you?
**Anne** I'm Anne Drayton. I'm Matthew's wife.
**Caroline** Oh. Oh, I see.

**Anne** I'm sorry, the front door was open. I——

**Caroline** Yes. I was—I was running—with a bottle for the phone. To answer the phone with a bottle. So I must have opened it and never shut it again.

**Anne** I see.

**Caroline** How did you know—what brings you here?

**Anne** Well, I knew about you. I saw you together one day.

**Caroline** And followed us?

**Anne** I did follow you, yes.

**Caroline** Why? I mean, if you're hoping to gain something. There's nothing to gain, you know.

**Anne** May I come in for a moment?

**Caroline** Yes. All right. I am expecting someone so I can't be too long.

**Anne** My husband?

**Caroline** No. Good Lord, no. No, I never expect him. No. We only meet for a lunch occasionally. He's one of many people I . . . Do sit down.

**Anne** Thank you.

**Caroline** What can I do for you, Mrs Drayton?

**Anne** Anne.

**Caroline** Yes, right.

**Anne** Caroline—it is Caroline, isn't it?

**Caroline** Possibly, yes.

**Anne** I came to warn you.

**Caroline** Warn me?

**Anne** Yes.

**Caroline** I see . . . I'm not going to be threatened. I'm sorry. I mean, I've lost a husband as well. I'm not unsympathetic but I'm not going to be threatened.

**Anne** Please. Would you listen to me, please? What I'm saying is—give him up before it's too late.

**Caroline** I'm sorry, I——

**Anne** He's an awful man. He'll destroy you. He really will.

**Caroline** Eh?

**Anne** He's a monster.

**Caroline** What on earth do you mean?

**Anne** He's really quite terrible, believe me. He's remorseless. He's unbending. He'll wear you down to nothing in no time, believe me.

**Caroline** Rubbish.

**Anne** You don't know him. You haven't lived with him. Nothing's ever right for him. Nothing.

**Caroline** Listen, I appreciate that you and he have had a tough time together . . .

**Anne** Have you ever done that silly thing with a piece of loose wool on a sweater? Pulled at it?

**Caroline** What are you talking about?

**Anne** A piece of wool at the bottom of a jumper or a sweater. It's hanging loose so you pull at it and if you pull long enough and hard enough, you finish up with a ball of wool and no jumper. That's what Matty does to you. He picks on a tiny fault, something quite trivial. He thinks your posture is wrong or you're a little overweight or you talk too much . . . a thousand things. But it doesn't stop there, he keeps going. Till you're frightened to move. Because everything—everything you do is wrong. Not just the way you're standing but the way you sit, the way you get in and out of a car, how you eat, how you drink, how you make love . . .

**Caroline** Yes. Mrs Drayton . . .

**Anne** (*going on remorselessly*) How you speak, how you cook—especially how you cook . . .

**Caroline** Mrs Drayton . . .

**Anne** He saps you, Caroline, he saps you . . .

**Caroline** (*firmly*) Mrs Drayton, I'm extremely sympathetic. I really am. It's obvious that you've had a terrible time. It's not that I disbelieve you, I don't. Something in you—some quality has obviously brought out something in Matthew. Maybe he did put on you—chivvy you but then maybe you asked for it . . .

**Anne** No, you don't understand, you really don't.

**Caroline** What I'm saying is that different things tend to happen between different people. You are obviously one of life's victims and I'm very, very sorry. But, thank God, Mrs Drayton, not all of us are made of wool.

### No. 25.   Caroline's Flat

*The Lights change*

**Anne** I had to leave him. My health was actually suffering. It wasn't that I wanted to leave. I had nothing to leave for. No job, no future, nobody else waiting, but I had to. For survival.

*Kevin enters with a bag from the bedroom*

**Kevin** I think that's everything.

**Caroline** (*to Kevin*) Right.

**Kevin** All of me is now packed.

**Anne** He kept gnawing away at you like a rodent. That's what he is, he's a rodent.

**Kevin** By tomorrow, you'll never know I existed. Not a trace.

**Caroline** The odd coffee stain on the carpet. Cigarette burns in the woodwork.

**Kevin** Won't let it drop, will you?

**Caroline** That's me. I can't change.

**Kevin** Normally I'd have said rubbish to that statement but in your case— no, I don't think you can change. But then you've never tried.

**Caroline** Have you?

**Kevin** Maybe not. But I've tried. I've tried to try.

**Caroline** I've made something to eat. Do you want it? Thought you might like a meal.

**Kevin** Starving actor? Yes, OK.

**Caroline** I'll get it on then. It won't take long. It's only bolognese. My usual. Is that OK?

**Kevin** Fine. Shall we have a drink then?

**Caroline** Sure.

**Kevin** Any beer left?

**Caroline** No, we've run out. I didn't . . .

**Kevin** Ah no. No point in getting any more, was there? Only you here to drink it.

**Caroline** Sherry. There's some sherry.

**Anne** You've obviously made up your mind that I'm here to wreck things somehow. Try and poison things between you. But why should I? I've got nothing to gain, have I?

**Caroline** (*handing Kevin a glass*) Here we are.

**Kevin** Thank you.

**Anne** I don't want him back.

**Kevin** Very civilized.

**Caroline** Well, we do try, don't we? I mean, there were moments when it became very, very difficult.

**Kevin** Like when you suddenly tried to claw my face off.

**Caroline** Or I find you in bed with one of my Sixth Formers.

**Kevin** Or when you attacked Joanna with watercress soup for no reason.

**Caroline** There was every reason for that . . .

**Kevin** And me coming home and finding Howard asleep on the sofa.

**Caroline** Now, I never went near him. You must believe that.

**Kevin** I believe that.

**Caroline** All right.

**Kevin** Right.

**Caroline** Quits then.

**Kevin** Quits. (*He sings*)

### No. 26.   Goodbye

As we sit here now
Like poker players
Who have stripped away
Their final layers
To reveal we're in a game nobody wins.

**Caroline**  We are on a road of no returning
Where the air is thick
With bridges burning
It is now the really painful part begins
For they haven't yet discovered
An easy way to say goodbye.

**Kevin**   *Adios.*                           **Caroline**  Toodle-oo.
*Sayonara.*                                  *Aloha.*
I'll be seeing you.                          Godspeed and *adieu.*
Fare thee well.
*Au revoir.*

| | |
|---|---|
| **Caroline** | Catchwords |
| | I hope will dry your tears and make it better |
| | I leave you with the spirit, not the letter |
| | I've no way |
| | Of saying |
| **Caroline** ⎫ **Kevin** ⎭ | Goodbye to you. |
| **Caroline** | We are one more pair |
| | Of weary dancers |
| | When we took the floor |
| | We hoped for answers |
| | Now we've asked the band to play our last request |
| **Kevin** | We are fools who've missed |
| | Their destination |
| | When we left the train |
| | They moved the station |
| | Is it any wonder now we need to rest? |
| | And we haven't yet discovered |
| | An easy way to say goodbye. |

*Matthew enters*

*He now echoes with Anne the sentiments of Caroline and Kevin*

| | | | |
|---|---|---|---|
| **Caroline** | *Adios.* | **Kevin** | *Wiedersehen.* |
| **Matthew** | *Sayonara.* | **Anne** | *Ciao*, so long. |
| **Caroline** | I'll be seeing you. | **Kevin** | *Vaya con dios.* |
| **Matthew** | Fare thee well. | | |
| **Caroline** | *Au revoir.* | | |

| | |
|---|---|
| **Kevin** | Stock words |
| | Impossible to give you any notion |
| | How perfectly they hide my true emotion. |
| | I've no way |
| | Of saying |
| **Kevin** ⎫ **Anne** ⎭ | Goodbye, my love. |
| **Caroline** ⎫ **Matthew** ⎭ | Goodbye, my love. |
| **Caroline** | Catchwords |
| | I hope will dry your tears and make it better |
| | I leave you with the spirit, not the letter. |
| **Anne** ⎫ **Kevin** ⎭ | There is no way I can say it |
| | Impossible to give you any notion |
| **Anne** ⎫ **Kevin** ⎬ **Matthew** ⎭ | Goodbye to you. |
| | How perfectly they hide my true emotion. |
| | Words can't say it. |
| **Caroline** ⎫ **Kevin** ⎭ | There is no way I can say it. |
| | How can I give an indication |
| | Of the way that I feel at our separation? |
| **Anne** | I hope will dry your tears and make it better |

| | |
|---|---|
| **Matthew** ⎫ | Goodbye to you. |
| ⎬ | Words can never say |
| **Caroline** ⎭ | How can I give an indication |
| | Of the way that I feel now that I'm leaving you? |
| **Anne** | I leave you with the spirit, not the letter. |
| **Matthew** ⎫ | Catchwords |
| | Impossible to give you any notion |
| ⎬ | How perfectly they hide my true emotion. |
| **Caroline** ⎪ | There is no way I can say it |
| **Anne** ⎭ | How can I give an indication |
| | Of the way that I feel at our separation? |
| **Kevin** ⎫ | Goodbye to you—words can't say it |
| **Caroline** ⎭ | How can I give an indication |
| | Of the way that I feel at our separation? |
| **Anne** ⎫ | There is no way I can say it |
| **Kevin** ⎭ | How can I give an indication |
| | Of the way that I feel at our separation? |
| **Caroline** | I hope will dry your tears and make it better. |
| **Anne** ⎫ | Goodbye to you—words can never say |
| **Matthew** ⎭ | How can I give an indication |
| | Now that I'm leaving you |
| **Caroline** | I leave you with the spirit, not the letter. |
| **Kevin** ⎫ | There's no way of saying to you |
| **Matthew** ⎭ | |
| **Caroline** ⎫ | No, we can't say |
| **Anne** ⎭ | |
| **All** | Goodbye. |

*At the end of the song the music restarts*

### No. 26A.  Goodbye (Reprise)

*The phone rings. The Lights reduce to the phone area*

   *Kevin, Matthew and Anne exit*

*Caroline answers the phone*

**Caroline** (*on the phone*) Sunday? . . . Yes, I'm clear. . . . No, it's only on Saturdays I've got my father to. . . . Yes. . . . why not? . . . let's go. . . . Whenever you like. . . . Oh, Matty, that's wonderful. . . . Yes, yes, yes . . .

*The Lights and the scene change. The music peaks*

*Caroline gathers up her coat as the scene changes*

   *Mathew enters with two suitcases and joins her*

*They are now standing in a hotel bedroom. Very two star. The music ends. They both stand staring round, Matthew holding the two suitcases*

**Matthew** Well, it's not quite what I had in mind but . . .

**Caroline** It's OK. It'll do. It's fine.

**Matthew** The chap who told me about this place drew a slightly rosier picture. There's damp coming in there. Look.

**Caroline** Oh well . . .

**Matthew** (*swinging the suitcases on to the bed*) Feel this bed.

**Caroline** (*at the window*) You can see the sea.

**Matthew** Can you?

**Caroline** Look.

**Matthew** (*joining her*) Where? Where's the sea? Can't see anything except a wall.

**Caroline** No, look if you . . . (*She twists, stands on tiptoe and cranes her neck to demonstrate*)

**Matthew** (*copying her*) Oh yes, so you can. Wow, what a view. Enough to send a giraffe into paroxysms of joy. I am sorry about this. It's not altogether my fault.

**Caroline** (*moving away from the window and hugging herself with cold*) Well . . .

**Matthew** And it is also very, very cold.

**Caroline** I don't care. I'm not going to let this get me down. This is the first time we've really been together for a whole uninterrupted evening. For a whole night. I'm going to enjoy it.

**Matthew** OK.

**Caroline** This is the new me. Positive me. Right. Do you want to go to bed now, please?

**Matthew** Now?

**Caroline** Be warmer.

**Matthew** Well, don't you want tea in the lounge first?

**Caroline** Couldn't we have that in bed?

**Matthew** (*doubtfully*) Well, I could ask that very old hall porter. The one I carried up the stairs carrying our luggage.

**Caroline** No, that's all right. Here's the plan then. We go down to the lounge, have tea, come up here again, go to bed, have fun, get up, get dressed, go down, have dinner, come up, have a cold bath, go to bed, have more fun, go to sleep. Does that sound OK?

**Matthew** You're unbelievably bouncy.

**Caroline** I'm very, very happy. Does it worry you? Me bouncing?

**Matthew** (*kissing her gently*) No.

**Caroline** Oh Matthew, I do love you.

**Matthew** Mmm.

**Caroline** Do you love me? At all?

**Matthew** What do you think?

**Caroline** Say it.

**Matthew** I love you.

**Caroline** A bit?

**Matthew** Quite a bit.

**Caroline** A lot?

**Matthew** Quite a lot.

**Caroline** Mmm. (*She cuddles up to him for a second*)

**Matthew** Do you want to unpack?

**Caroline** If you like. Oooh. It's cold, cold, cold . . . (*She jumps up and down*) This is a good way to keep warm. Do you mind if we make love like this? Jumping up and down. Pogo sex.

**Matthew** Well, there's no medical objection. You'll go through the floor, though.

**Caroline** No, I won't. It's very bouncy. Pogo, pogo, pogo.

*A banging on the ceiling. They both look up*

Oh Lord. Well, that's the end of that.

**Matthew** I'm glad to hear it. (*He opens one of the cases*)

**Caroline** I'll do that.

**Matthew** I just want my sweater.

**Caroline** (*opening her own case*) Look. (*She holds up a nightdress*) You like?

**Matthew** Very pretty.

**Caroline** I bought it for you. (*She holds it against her*) Look. Look. Do you like it?

**Matthew** (*putting on his sweater*) Rather.

**Caroline** I did anticipate the room being a fraction warmer, mind you. I may have to remain fully clothed underneath.

**Matthew** That's better. (*Picking up his spongebag*) I'll put this lot in the bathroom.

*Matthew goes off*

*Caroline picks up her coat, as if to hang it up. She is very happy. She wanders to the centre of the room*

### No. 27.   Scene Change

*The Lights change to past time. It is a sunny afternoon in the sitting-room o, her flat*

**Caroline** (*who has just apparently come in, yelling*) Kevin. Kev, are you in? Kev?

*Kevin appears in the bedroom doorway, in just his shirt, pants and socks*

**Kevin** (*sheepishly*) Hi.

**Caroline** Oh, you are in.

**Kevin** Hi.

**Caroline** You're not still in bed. It's five o'clcock. Have you been in bed all day?

**Kevin** Er—yes.

**Caroline** I don't believe it. Nobody needs that much sleep.

**Kevin** I thought you were staying in Bournemouth tonight?

**Caroline** (*idly tidying the room*) No, well, mother and I had one of our rows, so back I came. I can do without that . . . (*She breaks off*) Oh Kevin, really, look at this place . . . (*She breaks off*)

*She moves one of the sofa cushions and picks up a school dress*

(*Looking at it*) Oh God. (*She drops the dress and walks away*) You bastard. I don't believe it.

**Kevin** Er . . .

**Caroline** Get her out, Kevin. Whoever she is, get her out.

**Kevin** Look, Caroline——

**Caroline** (*fiercely*) Kevin, get her out of my bed, please.

*Caroline marches past Kevin to the bedroom door*

**Kevin** (*ineffectually, as she does so*) It's OK love, there's nothing to it . . .

*As Caroline arrives at the bedroom, Linda emerges from a corner of the room, draped in a sheet*

**Caroline** (*seeing her*) Oh, no.

**Linda** (*quite composed*) Good-afternoon, Mrs Hughes.

*Silence*

Excuse me. (*She passes them both, goes to the sofa and picks up her dress and other bits of clothing, including her bra*)

**Caroline** Oh, you're old enough to wear one of those now, are you, Linda? Jolly good.

*Linda looks daggers at her and goes*

**Kevin** Sorry, love. I'm sorry.

### No. 28.   Scene Change

**Caroline** Oh, Kevin . . .

**Kevin** (*uselessly*) Sorry. I'm just . . . Sorry.

*The music peaks and the Lights start to change back to the hotel*

(*As they do so*) Sorry . . . sorry . . . sorry . . .

*Kevin exits*

*Caroline now stands alone in the hotel room as before. The music finishes*

*Matthew returns still intent on unpacking*

**Matthew** (*as he enters and returns to his case*) What are you up to?

**Caroline** Oh, nothing. Nothing at all.

**Matthew** You're not considering starting pogoing again, are you?

*The music for "Risking" starts*

**Caroline** No. Given that up.

*She goes off to hang up her coat. She re-enters*

(*As she returns*) You're not going to believe this but I think they've got a tea dance downstairs.

**Matthew** Good Lord. How gruesome.

**Caroline** Matty . . .

**Matthew** Mmm?

**Caroline** I didn't tell you but—Anne's been to see me.

**Matthew** Anne? Who the hell's Anne?

**Caroline** She says she's your wife.

**Matthew** (*reacting sharply*) My wife's been to see you?

**Caroline** Yes.

**Matthew** How did she find you? How the hell did she find you?

**Caroline** She told me she followed us.

**Matthew** I knew it. She's got detectives out on me. I knew it.

**Caroline** I don't think it was detectives.

**Matthew** What did she want? What did she say to you?

**Caroline** Well, nothing. She went on about pullovers, mainly.

**Matthew** Pullovers?

**Caroline** She really hates you, doesn't she?

**Matthew** Yes. She does. Yes.

**Caroline** Is she—I hesitate to ask this but—is she slightly mentally unbalanced?

**Matthew** No. I don't—I wouldn't . . . She's very highly strung.

**Caroline** Oh yes.

**Matthew** What the hell was her game? Trying to wreck us, I suppose.

**Caroline** Poor woman.

**Matthew** Poor woman?

**Caroline** To feel like that. She must be really knotted up if she feels like that. Do you think I'll ever get like that?

**Matthew** No.

**Caroline** How do you know?

**Matthew** Because you're different. You're special.

**Caroline** Oh, Matty . . . (*She sings*)

### No. 29.  Risking

I was Miss Reliable
Or so they said
An upright little soul.
But now I'm Mistress Pliable
Who's lost her head
And blown her self-control.
There goes everything I had planned
Switching direction
Changing my tune
Look at the state of me
No more playing the one-man band.
As from this moment
Turning to you
Starting anew
Risking it all on love.

**Matthew**          It seemed unbelievable
To think that we

Could fall in love so soon.
At dawn the inconceivable
Was history
By early afternoon.
There go all of my careful schemes
Tear up the blueprints
Alter the plan
That's how it has to be.
All my future is based in dreams
I see the picture
How it will be
You here with me
Risking it all on love.

**Both**            There goes everything we had planned
Switching direction
Changing our tune
Look at the state of us
Two near strangers and here we stand
Starting together
Sharing the dance
Taking our chance
Risking it all on love.

*The song ends. Music continues under as Matthew kisses Caroline*

**Matthew**  Do you want to go downstairs?
**Caroline**  Downstairs?
**Matthew**  For tea? And dancing?
**Caroline**  What a terrible idea.
**Matthew**  Well then. You choose.
**Caroline**  I want to go to bed, please.
**Matthew**  All right. Let's go to bed.
**Caroline**  (*snatching up her sponge bag and nightdress*) Super. Right.

*She hurries towards the bathroom. The music ends*

   (*Stopping rather guiltily*) Are you in desperate need of tea?
**Matthew**  No.
**Caroline**  Yes, you are. You'd prefer tea. I can tell. You're looking very
   disappointed. You had your heart set on cucumber sandwiches and
   seed cake.
**Matthew**  Not at all.
**Caroline**  Come on, we'll go downstairs. It could be fun.
**Matthew**  Tell you what. I'll go down and get some. I'll bring it up on a
   tray.
**Caroline**  Are you allowed to do that?
**Matthew**  I don't think they can stop me really. I'll help myself. (*He moves
   to the door*)
**Caroline**  You better take the key. In case I'm in the bathroom.
**Matthew**  Thanks.

*Caroline goes to him, hands him the key and moves back to the bed*

**Caroline** Don't be long. (*Aware that Matthew is studying her*) What is it?
**Matthew** Just the way you stand.
**Caroline** How do you mean?
**Matthew** On the sides of your feet.
**Caroline** Do I? I didn't know.
**Matthew** Rather sweet. You walk that way, too.
**Caroline** Do I?
**Matthew** A bit.
**Caroline** Is that bad?
**Matthew** No, not at your age. Could be serious when you get older. Puts
a lot of unnecessary strain on the leg muscles, you see.
**Caroline** Oh . . .
**Matthew** Try shifting your weight over. Won't be a tick.

### No. 30.  Scene Change

*Matthew goes*

*Caroline practises a curious, compensatory walk. She stops and stares at her feet*

*Caroline goes off*

*The music peaks. The Lights change. It is still present time*

*Miss Dent enters*

**Miss Dent** Jumoke, will you come down off that at once, girl. It is out of
bounds and very dangerous . . . Yes, you—you, girl.

*Caroline dressed now in her coat and woolly hat comes and joins her*

**Caroline** (*rather breathless*) You wanted to see me, Miss Dent?
**Miss Dent** Oh, Caroline, dear—yes. Sorry to haul you away from things.
(*Indicating that they walk a little*) Shall we . . .?
**Caroline** Right.

*They both move away*

**Miss Dent** That's a pretty little hat.
**Caroline** Oh, yes. I'm just wearing it till I get it cut.
**Miss Dent** Mmm?
**Caroline** My hair. Not the hat.
**Miss Dent** (*laughing loudly*) You're going to have it short?
**Caroline** Yes. I've been told on good authority that it might help to im-
prove the shape of my face.
**Miss Dent** Your face?
**Caroline** Yes. It's apparently rather pear-shaped.
**Miss Dent** Is it? I never noticed. (*She peers at Caroline more closely*)
**Caroline** Apparently.

**Miss Dent** I don't think it's pear-shaped. Not really. Probably go that way in a few years, but give it a chance . . . (*Producing a bag of sweets from her pocket*) Will you . . .? No? . . . (*She takes one for herself*) Now, Caroline, I'm afraid I'm going to have to be a very boring acting headmistress for a minute.

**Caroline** Oh?

**Miss Dent** (*avoiding Caroline's gaze*) Yes, I wanted to ask you just before we break up for Christmas . . . I was going to ask you—I hope you don't take this the wrong way—but are you considering—regularizing your present private life a little?

**Caroline** Sorry?

**Miss Dent** You are still married, aren't you? That's the point. Technically.

**Caroline** Yes, I'm still married but I don't think that that. . . .

**Miss Dent** Nonetheless it is the case. You see, I have parents talking to me all the time and some of them, you know, I mean I'm Liberty Hall, you know me—you could live with the entire Fire Brigade for all I cared but——

**Caroline** No, I haven't divorced my husband. I haven't actually seen him to discuss it.

**Miss Dent** Oh dear. But I understand the person you're living with at present is also married?

**Caroline** Golly, yes. You have been doing your homework, Candida.

**Miss Dent** Well . . .

**Caroline** So you'd like me to put my house in order, is that it?

**Miss Dent** If you could see your way . . . I'd be grateful. It would take the pressure off me rather. I'm not . . . I hope you don't . . .

**Caroline** (*rather brusquely*) Well, I'll see what I can do, Candida.

**Miss Dent** You're looking very tired. Are you overdoing it?

**Caroline** (*moving off*) I must get back. I have a class.

**Miss Dent** Are you all right? You seem to be limping?

**Caroline** No, I'm fine. I'm just trying to correct my walk.

**Miss Dent** Is there something wrong with it?

**Caroline** Apparently, yes, apparently.

**Miss Dent** Oh dear. I should see a doctor.

**Caroline** I do. Frequently. What with that and my big fat face, I've rather got my hands full at the moment. Good-afternoon.

*She goes off*

**Miss Dent** (*faintly*) Goodbye. (*To herself*) I do hope she's all right.

*Miss Dent exits*

## No. 31.  Scene Change

*The Lights cross fade back to the sitting-room of Caroline's flat. It is present time*

*Caroline enters from the kitchen, now hatless. She carries a Christmas*

*tree (a small, artificial one) and two brightly wrapped parcels. She puts
them down on the table*

*The doorbell rings*

**Caroline** OK. I'm coming. Just a sec.

*She goes into the hall*

(*Off*) So I'm not the only one who leaves his front-door key behind, am
I? Oh. Come in.

*She re-enters with Howard. He is in his overcoat and hat. He carries a
bunch of flowers*

**Howard** Hallo. I don't know if you—if you even remember me but . . .

**Caroline** Yes, of course. It's—it's Howard, isn't it?

**Howard** That's right, yes.

**Caroline** Howard-er . . .

**Howard** Potter.

**Caroline** Potter, yes. Well, this is a surprise.

**Howard** Pretty ridiculous idea really. I mean, it's been years hasn't it?
Two or three. And then, I don't know, I started thinking about you and
then, by some strange coincidence, I ran into your Kevin. Your husband.
In this restaurant and . . . Or is he your ex-husband?

**Caroline** No. Husband.

**Howard** And he said you were . . . And I thought the chances are you'll
be . . . but then again perhaps . . . so, being Christmas, I thought why not.
See if you're still around. Possibly even—if you fancy it—take you out
to dinner. Make up for last time.

**Caroline** Last time?

**Howard** When we both missed it. At Ivor's. Remember?

**Caroline** Oh, yes.

**Howard** I know what it is. About this room.

**Caroline** What?

**Howard** You've moved all the furniture round, that's what's different.

**Caroline** No it was moved—by a friend. A friend rearranged it. It's better
—proportionately . . .

**Howard** Oh. Is it?

**Caroline** Apparently. Yes.

**Howard** (*unconvinced*) Oh. Well. So what do you say? Dinner? You look
as if you could do with a good meal, if you don't mind my saying so.
You look a bit thin in the face.

**Caroline** Oh. Do I?

**Howard** What do you say?

*Matthew enters. He carries his briefcase and two gift-wrapped parcels*

**Matthew** Front door's wide open, darling, are you . . .? (*Seeing Howard*)
Oh, hallo.

**Howard** Ah.

**Caroline** Matthew, this is Howard Potter. An old friend from way back.
Just looked in to say Happy Christmas. This is Matthew Drayton.

**Howard** How do you do.

**Matthew** Glad to meet you. Would you care for a drink?

**Howard** No, no, no. I must be off. I only really stuck my head literally round the door to say hallo to—er—to—Coral.

**Caroline** Caroline.

**Howard** Caroline.

**Matthew** If you're sure.

**Howard** No. I have to take these flowers round to my mother. And er— good to see you again, Caroline. Cheerio.

**Caroline** Yes, I hope so.

**Matthew** Yes, right. I'll . . . (*He makes to show him out*)

**Howard** No, I'll shut my own door. Don't worry. Goodbye.

**Matthew** Goodbye.

**Caroline** Goodbye.

*Howard hurries out*

**Matthew** Odd bloke.

**Caroline** Yes, he is quite odd, I suppose.

**Matthew** Where do you know him from?

**Caroline** Met him at Jilly's, I think.

**Matthew** Oh, yes? Might have guessed. Right, everything under control?

**Caroline** I don't think so.

**Matthew** Made us a drink?

**Caroline** 'Fraid not.

**Matthew** Got the dinner on?

**Caroline** Not yet. I didn't know what time you'd——

**Matthew** Made the bed?

**Caroline** No.

**Matthew** My God. What have you been doing all day, girl?

**Caroline** Nothing.

**Matthew** (*giving her a hug*) I don't know. How did you manage before I met you, eh? Dozy ha'porth. (*Kissing her*) Happy Christmas.

**Caroline** (*dully*) Happy Christmas.

**Matthew** I'll get us a drink. (*He moves away, then turns back to look at her*) What's the matter?

**Caroline** Nothing.

**Matthew** Come on, you're looking depressed again.

**Caroline** No, I'm not. I was just thinking, that's all.

**Matthew** Now, remember what I told you about these depressions. You must not let them get hold of you.

**Caroline** I am not depressed, Matt, I'm just thinking. That's all. And, occasionally, when I think my face muscles tend to forget to hold up my big heavy jaw on my big heavy face.

**Matthew** You're getting a thing about your face, you know. You'd better watch it. Nothing more boring than women who bleat on about their faces for hours on end. Becoming a phobia.

## No. 32.   Scene Change

*Matthew goes out*

*Caroline makes a strange gurgling sound which could be a scream. The Lights change. We are back in past time*

*Kevin stands in the doorway*

**Kevin** I don't know how I forgot. I'm sorry.
**Caroline** OK.
**Kevin** I didn't know it was your birthday.
**Caroline** Obviously not.
**Kevin** Or I'd have bought you something. You should have reminded me.
**Caroline** Yes, I'm very sorry I forgot, Kevin. I'll try to remember in future.
**Kevin** Yes, well.
**Caroline** It doesn't matter.
**Kevin** I'm afraid I haven't told you the worst.
**Caroline** What?
**Kevin** I spilt red wine on your sofa last night.
**Caroline** (*alarmed*) Oh no, where?
**Kevin** (*indicating*) There. I covered it up with a cushion. I don't think there's anything you can do. Sorry.

*He goes out shaking his head*

**Caroline** I can't bear it, Kevin, I really can't. If you've ruined this as well as everything . . . (*she picks up the cushion and her voice tails off. She has found a small gift-wrapped parcel*) What is . . .? (*Screaming*) Kevin, that is a rotten bloody joke!

## No. 33.   Scene Change

*A yell of mirth from the kitchen*

That is just not funny, Kevin. (*She sits on the sofa and swings her feet up*)

*The Lights change back to present time*

*Matthew returns, carrying two glasses of sherry*

**Matthew** Right. Is it time for the presents?
**Caroline** If you like.

*She catches his expression of disapproval*

I mean, yes. Super, super. (*She smiles glazedly and kicks her feet*)
**Matthew** I wouldn't do that with your shoes on, you'll ruin your sofa.
**Caroline** Goody.
**Matthew** (*choosing to ignore this*) What's the idea of opening our presents on Christmas Eve?
**Caroline** It's a family tradition.
**Matthew** In your family?

**Caroline** Yes.

**Matthew** How did that come about?

**Caroline** I started it.

**Matthew** Why?

**Caroline** Because I couldn't wait till Christmas Day.

**Matthew** Oh, I see. You were indulged as a child, too, were you? Explains a lot.

**Caroline** (*giving him another awful smile*) Yes, doesn't it?

**Matthew** I'm not going to have that all over Christmas, am I?

**Caroline** We shall see. That is from me to you. And that is from me to you. (*She hands him two parcels*)

**Matthew** I mean, if you're spoiling for an argument, you might at least let me know what it's about.

**Caroline** No argument. Are those for me? (*She indicates his two parcels*)

**Matthew** Yes. There. (*He tosses them over rather ungraciously*)

**Caroline** Thank you so much. Happy Christmas.

**Matthew** And to you.

**Caroline** Thanks. Now, what have we got here? (*She rips open her parcel almost savagely*)

*Matthew does the same. They are neither enjoying themselves*

I can't think what it is.

**Matthew** Oh, that one's just a joke.

**Caroline** (*finally unwrapping a book from her parcel and reading the title*) *A Hundred Ways To Keep Fit.* Oh yes, that's a super joke.

*Matthew opens his present*

**Matthew** Ah.

**Caroline** Those aren't a joke, I'm afraid. They were extremely expensive.

**Matthew** Cuff links.

**Caroline** Yes.

**Matthew** Lovely. We must go out and buy a few shirts that need them. All my cuffs have buttons.

**Caroline** Don't worry. I'll rip them off for you, if you like. (*Opening her other parcel*) Oh now, look at this.

**Matthew** Now that was expensive.

**Caroline** A whole herbal beauty treatment. Just for me and my big body. Is there enough to cover it, I ask myself?

**Matthew** (*grimly*) This one mine?

**Caroline** I think it must be.

**Matthew** Thank you. (*He starts to open it*)

**Caroline** Don't you dare complain about that. That wasn't just expensive. It was very, very expensive. I went to a lot of trouble for that.

*Matthew unwraps an expensive cardigan*

**Matthew** (*studying it*) Yes. Yes. Beautifully styled.

**Caroline** Isn't it?

**Matthew** Yes.

**Caroline** What about that colour?

**Matthew** Yes.

**Caroline** It'll suit you.

**Matthew** I'm not sure it would, actually, darling.

**Caroline** Of course it will. It's absolutely you.

**Matthew** Well, I think I must beg to differ. I do know my own colouring,
   I think, by now. And I do know which colours happen to suit me.

**Caroline** Dull ones.

**Matthew** Not always.

**Caroline** So you don't like that?

**Matthew** It's lovely but . . .

**Caroline** Fine. Let's have it. I'll give it to the Scouts. Or, better still, you
   keep it and unravel it when you get bored.

**Matthew** Oh, now don't be stupid.

**Caroline** You only don't like it because I didn't leap in the air with joy
   over your bloody herbal beauty treatment.

**Matthew** I thought you might have shown a little pleasure. I went to a lot
   of trouble.

**Caroline** So did I. Do you know how much that cost me?

**Matthew** All right. That was extremely expensive too, as it happens.

**Caroline** Oh was it?

**Matthew** As it happens, yes it was. Would you care to see the receipt? I
   still have the receipt.

**Caroline** (*rising*) Ah, well now. If we're going to start showing receipts. I
   can show you receipts.

**Matthew** All right, all right.

**Caroline** Well, I'm sorry. I am not a woman who starts doing cartwheels
   when someone gives her a load of beauty treatments. Nor am I going to
   scream with delight at a book full of pictures of emaciated middle-aged
   women in gym vests. I'm a teacher, for God's sake. I seem to spend my
   life surrounded by women jumping about in vests.

**Matthew** I don't know what you're talking about.

**Caroline** I'm talking about you. Being too mean to give me any real
   presents. Instead you give me gift-wrapped hints.

**Matthew** You're beyond me. Totally beyond me. You're incapable, aren't
   you, of taking the teeniest little bit of criticism?

**Caroline** Teeny? Did you say teeny criticism? Would you like the list?
   All right, have the list. My feet are wrong. My hair's wrong. My bottom's
   too big. I'm colour blind. Tone deaf. My nose is wrong. My ears are
   crooked. My tits are lopsided . . .

**Matthew** Please keep your voice down. Don't screech.

**Caroline** Oh, yes, I'm sorry. My voice is squeaky. My furniture's in the
   wrong place.

**Matthew** Stop shouting.

**Caroline** My cooking is inedible.

**Matthew** Stop shouting now.

**Caroline** Particularly my spaghetti bolognese of which I happen to be
   extremely proud.

**Matthew** (*getting louder*) Caroline, will you please stop shouting?

**Caroline** This is my flat. Why the hell shouldn't I shout? I'll shout if I want to.

**Matthew** (*shouting her down*) Will you shut up? Will you shut up and pull yourself together, woman!

**Caroline** (*loudly*) What? (*Slight pause. Then quieter*) What?

*They both stand slightly breathless and exhausted*

**Matthew** (*with great self-control*) Look, I'm sorry. I don't know what I've done to deserve that outburst. I really don't. The point is I'm not prepared to put up with it. I'm sorry. (*Thinking things through*) Now, talking about this calmly it seems—apparently—something I am doing or saying is causing you to react in this uncontrolled and unstable manner. I've no idea, quite frankly, what it can be. To be honest, I think it's probably something more in your mind than anywhere else.

**Caroline** (*growing angry again*) In my . . . My God, he's starting on my mind now.

**Matthew** (*cutting her off*) Caroline! (*Quietly*) This is what I think we should do. I'm going to put my front door key of the flat here on the table, like this. (*He does so*) And I'm going out for a short walk. I propose to cool down, before I start saying things to you that I'll regret. Might I suggest you do the same? In ten minutes or so, I shall be back and I shall ring the bell. The choice is then yours. You may open the door to me and accept that we carry on as we are. Or else, you can choose to leave it closed. If you do that, it will be the last you'll ever see of me. Does that seem fair?

**Caroline** (*nodding mutely*) All right.

**Matthew** Sure?

**Caroline** OK.

**Matthew** Think it over. I won't be long.

*He moves to the front door*

**Caroline** (*in a small voice*) Matty?

**Matthew** Yes.

**Caroline** You'd really leave? Just like that?

**Matthew** It's up to you to choose, Caroline. It's your life as well. And I've never wanted to interfere with that. As I think you know . . . I'll see you in a minute. I'm sure I will.

*He goes*

*Caroline is totally lost*

**Caroline** Oh. (*She dithers*) Well, I don't know. Do I? I don't know. (*Calling*) Matty? What do I do? Matty? Jilly? Ivor? Kev? Somebody? Anyone? Please? (*She sings*)

### No. 34. Individual

*The brace in the left-hand margin indicates ensemble singing*

I think like me
'Cos I'm an

Individual
Don't you try and alter me.
I'm stuck like this
And this is how I plan to be
At least
It's mine.
That suits me fine.
And you won't change
This dogged
Individual
You gotta take me warts and all
I've got my faults
But they're the nicest part of me.
This is
Your lot
Me's all I've got.
I'd hate to give you the false impression
I'm about to improve
You'll have to settle for this
If you're hoping to do better
Though I wouldn't want to stop you
And you're welcome to try
This is something special
That you're kissing goodbye
One of a kind . . .
Here I am, a bargain offering
Completely custom-made
Full of flaws and British workmanship
I've everything displayed.
That you ridicule my intellect, I tell from
      your tone
Grubbing in your greenhouse, looking round
      for a stone
Watch where it's thrown
I have my own supply.
I don't bow down to any old authority
Superiority
Stuff your seniority
So watch your step
'Cos I'm an individual
One off
That's me—Just wait and see.

*The music continues. The doorbell rings. Then a knocking on the door.
Matthew's muffled voice is heard, presumably through the letter-box*

**Matthew** (*speaking, off*) Caroline? Caroline, open up, it's only me.
   Matthew. Come on, let me in, Caroline. (*Knocking again*) Please,
   Caroline. Caroline, my briefcase is in there. (*More knocking*)

*During the following, Caroline empties Matthew's briefcase into the air and generally begins to untidy the flat*

**Caroline** (*singing*) I don't take kindly to polite suggestions
I could mend and make do—
I'm far too old to reform
If you're itching to remould me
Well, apart from your obtrusiveness
To which I'm averse,
There's a possibility
You're making me worse.
Go catch a hearse.
You should know there's only one of me,
Our number's in decline.
An endangered species possibly
The last one in a line.
No, you couldn't be more wrong about me,
Not if you tried
Take it from the person who is living inside
I must confide
I have my pride—like you.
So, stand well clear,
'Cos I'm an individual
Individual
Answering to nobody
I won't change you
'Cos you're an individual
You're not—like me
So be yourself.

*The Company enter and sing*

| **1st Company** | **Caroline** |
|---|---|
| Give me air, | Give me air, |
| Here comes an individual | So I can be myself, |
| Individual | I'm quite unmistakably |
| Answering to nobody. | So individually me. |
| I won't change you | Won't change you |
| 'Cos you're an individual. | You're you. |
| **2nd Company** | |
| Just be you | |
| Individual | |
| You | |
| Girl | |
| Just be you. | |
| **1st Company** You're not | |
| **2nd Company** You're not | I'm me |
| **1st Company** Like me | |
| **2nd Company** Like me | Like you |

| | | |
|---|---|---|
| **1st Company** | So be— | |
| | —yourself | Somebody special |
| **Company** | Just— | I need more room |
| | —be— | 'Cos I'm an individual. |
| | —you. | |
| | All together now | All together now |
| | Yourself | Answering to nobody. |
| | Just— | I won't change you |
| | —be— | 'Cos you're an individual. |
| | —you. | |
| **Caroline** | You're like | |
| **Company** | You're like | |
| **Caroline** | Yourself | |
| **Company** | Yourself | |
| **Caroline** | So be like | |
| **Company** | Yourself | |
| **Caroline** | You be like | |
| **Company** | Like you like | |
| **Caroline** | I'll be like | |
| **Caroline** } | I like to . . . | |
| **Company** } | | |

*Caroline cries out. The Lights change to a solo spot on Caroline*

   *A spot comes up on Jilly standing in an entrance*

**Jilly** (*on echo*) Caroline . . .

   *A spot comes up on Ivor*

**Ivor** (*on echo*) Hallo, Caroline. Brought your milk in again.

**Jilly** (*on echo*) It's the same old story, isn't it? What have you been drinking this time?

**Ivor** (*on echo*) There's a roast turkey out here, you know, Bubbles. In the middle of the kitchen table. Brussel sprouts. Roast potatoes, chestnut stuffing, cranberry sauce . . .

   *Ivor goes*

**Jilly** (*echo*) Caroline . . . old friend to see you . . .

   *Jilly goes*

*Caroline waits apprehensively*

   *A spot comes up on Howard*

**Howard** (*echo*) Hallo, Coral. You won't remember me but . . .

   *Howard goes*

**Jilly** (*off, echo*) . . . old friend to see you . . .

   *A spot comes on Matthew*

**Matthew** (*echo*) Caroline, let me in, it's Matthew . . .

*Matthew goes*

**Jilly** (*off*, *echo*) . . . old friend to see you . . .

*A spot comes up on Kevin*

**Kevin** (*echo*) Hallo. Making a habit of this, aren't I?

*Kevin goes*

**Jilly** (*off*, *echo*) . . . old friend to see you . . .

*A spot comes up on Matthew*

**Matthew** (*echo*) . . . come along, darling, pull yourself together . . .

*Matthew goes*

**Jilly** (*off*, *echo*) . . . old friend to see you . . .

*A spot comes up on Kevin*

**Kevin** (*echo*) Me again. Caroline . . . ?

*Kevin goes*

*A spot comes up on Naylor Page*

**Naylor** (*echo*) Hallo, remember me? Naylor Page?

*Naylor goes*

**Linda** (*off*, *echo*) Miss Baxter, Miss Baxter.
**Ivor** (*off*, *echo*, *under the next*) Caroline . . . Caroline . . . Caroline . . .
(*etc*)

*A spot comes up on Matthew*

**Matthew** (*echo*) Caroline, my briefcase is in there.

*A spot comes up on Kevin*

**Kevin** (*echo*) Caroline . . . Caroline . . .

*Kevin goes*

**Anne** (*off*, *echo*) He saps you, Caroline, he saps you.

*A spot comes up on Douglas*

**Douglas** (*echo*) The only thing wrong with you, girl, the only thing wrong with you . . .

*Douglas goes*

*A spot comes up on Matthew*

**Matthew** (*echo*) Pogo! Pogo! Pogo!

*Matthew goes*

*Echo off, Joanna laughs under the next*

    *A spot comes up on Kevin who is carrying a box of chocolates*

**Kevin** (*echo*) Caroline . . .

    *A spot comes up on Naylor*

**Naylor** (*echo*) Fork lift trucks, Carol . . .
**Miss Dent** (*off, echo*) Caroline, will you come down off that at once, girl.

    *A spot comes up on Matthew*

*Caroline starts to sing, softly at first, as Kevin, Miss Dent, Matthew and Naylor speak the following together*

**Kevin**
    (*echo*) Caroline . . . Caroline . . .
    Caroline . . . (*etc.*)
**Miss Dent**
    (*off, echo*) That is out of bounds
    and extremely dangerous . . .
**Matthew**
    (*echo*) You're incapable, aren't
    you, of taking the teeniest
    little bit of criticism?
**Naylor**
    (*echo*) It's got this new roof line
    and three-quarter vents . . . (*etc.*)

**Caroline** (*singing*)
Individual
You gotta take me warts
  and all
I've got my faults
But they're the nicest part
  of me

(*She gets louder*)
This is
Your lot

(*Shouting*)
Me's all I've got.

*Silence*

    *Matthew and Naylor exit*

**The Lights come up on Caroline and Kevin, now alone in the sitting-room**

**Kevin** (*gently*) Caroline.
**Caroline** Oh.
**Kevin** Hallo.
**Caroline** Hallo. Well.
**Kevin** Yes, I heard on the grapevine you were back on your own. So I rang the school. But they said you were away. Which seemed odd. So I —thought I'd look in. See if you were coping.
**Caroline** I'm fine.
**Kevin** Managing OK?
**Caroline** Oh, yes. Everything's under control.
**Kevin** (*surveying the debris*) Yes. Yes, I can see. (*He sits on the sofa*) You're looking a bit thin.
**Caroline** Oh. And you? What's been happening to you?
**Kevin** Nothing much. I've been fairly busy. Workwise.
**Caroline** Yes, I saw you once or twice.

**Kevin** (*shifting the book he is sitting on*) *A Hundred Ways To Keep Fit.*
Have you been doing these?
**Caroline** No, that's a joke.
**Kevin** Really? (*Mirthlessly*) Ha ha.

*The music for "Caroline's Answers" (Reprise) starts*

(*Opening the chocolate box*) These look rather good, you know. Want
one?
**Caroline** Oh, Kev . . .
**Kevin** Mmm?
**Caroline** Kev . . . (*She runs to him and hugs him*) I'm sorry.
**Kevin** (*hugging her*) No. I'm sorry.
**Caroline** (*gripping him tightly*) Oh, I love you. I love you. I love you.
**Kevin** (*trying to move*) Aaah.
**Caroline** What?
**Kevin** Sorry. I think we're grinding chocolate into your sofa.
**Caroline** Oh, bugger the sofa. (*She clings on to him. She sings*)

### No. 35.   Caroline's Answers (Reprise)

Could it be this is an answer?
Far too soon to tell.
All I am completely sure is—
Nothing's really known.
Why not choose myself an ending
Where at least I'm not alone?
For happiness is something
That is never yours by right.
Why not settle for today
And cuddle up tonight?

*The Lights fade to Black-out*

# FURNITURE AND PROPERTY LIST

Please see the Author's Note on page v concerning the staging of the original production. Settings will have to be adapted to suit the individual staging facilities available and therefore only essential items are given in this list but further dressing may be added at the director's discretion. Again, for the scene changes sets will have to be struck and re-set according to the facilities available, and, apart from the opening sets for Acts I and II, all furniture is listed as off stage and it is assumed this will be set by the stage management as will all properties which do not have a character's name after them in brackets.

## ACT I

**The Sitting-Room**

*On stage:* Table
Chair
Sofa. *On it:* cushions, clothes, papers, books etc.
Phone
Record player
Glass for **Caroline**
Used cups and saucers, books etc. scattered about the floor
**Caroline's** shoes

*Off stage:* Newspapers **(Jilly)**
Large number of full milk bottles **(Ivor)**
Tray. *On it:* three cups and saucers, teapot with tea **(Ivor)**

**The Main School Entrance**

**Caroline's** raincoat **(Linda)**

**The Restaurant**

Table
Two chairs

**The Classroom**

Gift-wrapped parcel containing a book of love poems **(Linda)**

### The Sitting-Room

Table
Chair
Sofa. *On it:* cushions
Phone
Record player
Gift-wrapped parcel containing a book of love poems **(Caroline)**


### The School Corridor

Nil


### The Party

Glass **(Joanna)**
Glass **(Kevin)**


### The Sitting-Room

Table
Chair
Sofa. *On it:* cushions, **Caroline's** dressing-gown
Phone
Record player
Box of chocolates **(Miss Dent)**
Can of beer **(Kevin)**


### The Kitchen

Table. *On it:* books, exercise books etc.
Two chairs
Fridge (practical). *In it:* cans of beer
Table cloth **(Caroline)**
Bag. *In it:* copy of Milton with piece of paper containing a poem,
    exercise books etc. **(Linda)**


### The Tobacconist And Newsagent Shop

Racks of magazines
Cup of tea **(Caroline)**

### The Sitting-Room

Table
Chair
Sofa. *On it:* cushions, other items, book of love poems, **Caroline's**
    handbag containing mirror, make-up, dark glasses
Phone
Record player
Dress **(Caroline)**
Envelope **(Linda)**
Flannel **(Caroline)**

### The Bathroom Area

Mirror
Razor
Sticking plaster

### The Dining-Room

Table. *On it:* six place settings, opened bottle of wine, six glasses, dish
    of raw vegetable cruditées, plates etc.
Six chairs
Glass of drink **(Jilly)**
Bowl of taramasalata **(Ivor)**

*Personal:* **Ivor:** apron

## ACT II

### The Dining-Room

*On stage:* Table. *On it:* six place settings, opened bottle of wine, six glasses, six
    soup bowls
    Six chairs

*Off stage:* Glass of drink **(Jilly)**
    Tureen of soup with ladle **(Ivor)**
    Six plates **(Jilly)**
    Hot vegetable dish **(Howard)**
    Steaming serving dish **(Ivor)**

*Personal:* **Ivor:** apron
    **Kevin:** sticking plaster
    **Caroline:** dark glasses

### The Sitting-Room

*Off stage:*   Table
             Chair
             Sofa. *On it:* cushions, other items
             Phone
             Record player
             Glasses
             Bottle of sherry
             Milk bottle **(Howard)**
             Cup of coffee **(Howard)**
             Two cups of coffee **(Matthew)**
             **Joanna's** soup-stained dress **(Kevin)**
             Bottle of brandy **(Caroline)**
             Bag **(Kevin)**

*Personal:*   **Howard:** wallet
             **Joanna:** handbag containing a key

### The Hotel Bedroom

*Off stage:*   Bed
             Two suitcases. In **Caroline's:** nightdress. In **Matthew's:** sweater,
             spongebag **(Matthew)**

### The Sitting-Room

Table
Chair
Sofa. *On it:* cushions with school dress, bra, etc. hidden behind them
Phone
Record player

### The Hotel Bedroom

Bed. *On it:* nightdress, hotel key, two opened suitcases. In **Caroline's**
case: spongebag

### The School

*Personal:*   **Miss Dent:** bag of sweets in her pocket

### The Sitting-Room (*A few items are arranged differently to before*)

*Off stage:*   Table
             Chair
             Sofa. *On it:* cushions
             Phone
             Record player

Small artificial Christmas tree, brightly wrapped parcel containing a pair of cuff links, brightly wrapped parcel containing an expensive cardigan **(Caroline)**

Bunch of flowers **(Howard)**

Briefcase containing various items, gift-wrapped copy of "A Hundred Ways To Keep Fit", gift-wrapped herbal beauty treatment **(Matthew)**

**During music No 32. "Scene Change"**

*Set:*    Small gift-wrapped parcel behind a sofa cushion

**During music No 33. "Scene Change"**

*Strike:*    Small gift-wrapped parcel

*Off stage:* Two glasses of sherry **(Matthew)**
Box of chocolates **(Kevin)**

# LIGHTING PLOT

Practical fittings required: fridge
Various interior and exterior settings

## ACT I

*To open:*   Gloomy winter afternoon effect

*Cue 1*   **Jilly** enters the sitting-room and switches on the lights                     (Page 1)
*Bring up interior lighting*

*Cue 2*   **Caroline** (*singing*): "And so alone at night."                     (Page 9)
*Change to summer evening effect*

*Cue 3*   **Kevin** goes off removing his jacket to the hall                     (Page 9)
*Change back to interior lighting*

*Cue 4*   **Caroline** removes the phone from the hook                     (Page 10)
*Change to exterior summer late afternoon effect*

*Cue 5*   **Kevin:** "My pleasure."                     (Page 11)
*Change to interior lighting effect on restaurant table*

*Cue 6*   **Caroline** and **Kevin** get up from the table                     (Page 12)
*Cross fade to classroom area*

*Cue 7*   **Caroline** and **Linda** exit. The music changes                     (Page 12)
*Cross fade to the sitting-room area to give a bright summer sunlight effect*

*Cue 8*   **Kevin:** "Oh right." (The music peaks)                     (Page 13)
*Cross fade to the school corridor*

*Cue 9*   The music changes to party/disco type music                     (Page 14)
*Cross fade to separate area to give interior lighting effect*

*Cue 10*   **Caroline** stands scowling. The party music swells                     (Page 15)
*Cross fade to the sitting-room to give a gloomy effect*

*Cue 11*   **Miss Dent:** "We were so happy."                     (Page 17)
*Slowly change to give a summer evening effect*

*Cue 12*   **Joanna** enters                     (Page 18)
*Spot on **Joanna**. Fade as she exits*

*Cue 13*   **Joanna** enters                     (Page 18)
*Spot on **Joanna**. Fade as she exits*

*Cue 14*   **Joanna** enters                     (Page 20)
*Spot on **Joanna**. Fade as she exits*

*Cue 15*   **Kevin** exits                     (Page 21)
*Cross fade to the kitchen area to give summer evening effect*

*Cue 16*   **Kevin** goes out                     (Page 26)
*Cross fade to tobacconist shop to give interior effect*

| | | |
|---|---|---|
| *Cue* 17 | Everyone exits at the end of song No. 11<br>*Cross fade to sitting-room to give summer evening effect* | (Page 28) |
| *Cue* 18 | **Caroline** picks up her dress and examines it<br>*Bring up summer evening effect in the bathroom area* | (Page 32) |
| *Cue* 19 | When ready<br>*Bring up interior lighting effect on dining-room* | (Page 34) |
| *Cue* 20 | **Matthew** (*speaking*): "Absolutely first rate."<br>*Dim lighting to spot on* **Caroline** | (Page 38) |
| *Cue* 21 | **Caroline** (*singing*): "And so alone at——"<br>*Change back to previous lighting* | (Page 39) |
| *Cue* 22 | **Ivor** (*speaking*): "A toast to Jilly."<br>*Dim lighting to spot on* **Caroline** | (Page 40) |
| *Cue* 23 | **Caroline** (*singing*): ". . . or a tactful no?"<br>*Change back to previous lighting* | (Page 40) |
| *Cue* 24 | **Caroline** and **Matthew** look at each other<br>*Lights fade to Black-out* | (Page 41) |

## ACT II

| | | |
|---|---|---|
| *To open:* | Summer evening light | |
| *Cue* 25 | **Kevin** (*speaking*): "All the best, mate."<br>*Dim lighting to spot on* **Caroline** | (Page 46) |
| *Cue* 26 | **Caroline** (*singing*): "And sleep alone at——"<br>*Change back to previous lighting* | (Page 46) |
| *Cue* 27 | **Kevin** (*speaking*): "All the best, Jilly."<br>*Dim lighting to spot on* **Caroline** | (Page 48) |
| *Cue* 28 | **Caroline** (*singing*): "Losing her restraint."<br>*Change back to previous lighting* | (Page 48) |
| *Cue* 29 | **Ivor**: "Eh?" (The music peaks)<br>*Cross fade to give dark effect in the sitting-room* | (Page 52) |
| *Cue* 30 | **Caroline** switches on the lights<br>*Bring up interior lighting* | (Page 52) |
| *Cue* 31 | **Caroline**: "With fascinating people like me . . ."<br>*Change to give summer late evening effect* | (Page 54) |
| *Cue* 32 | **Howard** goes back into the kitchen<br>*Change to interior lighting effect as in Cue 30* | (Page 55) |
| *Cue* 33 | **Caroline**: "Good heavens . . ."<br>*Change to summer late evening effect, growing darker* | (Page 55) |
| *Cue* 34 | **Caroline** puts the coffee cup down<br>*Change to interior lighting effect as before* | (Page 56) |
| *Cue* 35 | **Kevin** and **Joanna** enter a separate area<br>*Bring up spot on* **Kevin** *and* **Joanna**. *Fade as they exit* | (Page 58) |
| *Cue* 36 | **Caroline** exits<br>*Fade down and then bring up winter afternoon effect* | (Page 59) |

*Cue* 37    **Anne:** "For survival."                                          (Page 61)
             *Change to summer light effect*

*Cue* 38    Phone rings                                                         (Page 64)
             *Reduce lighting to phone area*

*Cue* 39    **Caroline:** ". . . Yes, yes, yes . . ."                           (Page 64)
             *Bring up gloomy wintry light effect in hotel bedroom*

*Cue* 40    **Caroline** wanders to the centre of the room                      (Page 66)
             *Cross fade to give sunny afternoon effect in the sitting-room*

*Cue* 41    The music peaks                                                     (Page 67)
             *Lights change slowly to give gloomy wintry effect in hotel*
                *bedroom*

*Cue* 42    **Caroline** goes off. The music peaks                              (Page 70)
             *Cross fade to separate area to give exterior winter daylight*
                *effect*

*Cue* 43    **Miss Dent** exits                                                 (Page 71)
             *Cross fade to sitting-room to give gloomy, wintry effect*

*Cue* 44    **Matthew** goes out                                                (Page 74)
             *Change to summer light effect*

*Cue* 45    **Caroline** sits on the sofa and swings her feet up                (Page 74)
             *Change back to gloomy wintry effect*

*Cue* 46    **Caroline** cries out                                              (Page 80)
             *Dim lighting to a spot on* **Caroline**

*Cues*      On pages 80 to 82 a lighting change is indicated each time
47–60       a character appears and exits. This may be done with
             either a spot over two of the entrances which alternate
             as the characters come and go, or, if facilities do not
             permit this, one spot could be used with the characters
             stepping in and out of the light in turn. Please refer to
             these pages for the cues

*Cue* 61    **Matthew** and **Naylor** exit                                     (Page 82)
             *Bring up gloomy wintry effect on sitting-room*

*Cue* 62    **Caroline** (*singing*): "And cuddle up tonight?"                  (Page 83)
             *Fade to Black-out*

# EFFECTS PLOT

**ACT I**

| | | |
|---|---|---|
| *Cue 1* | After the doorbell has rung 2nd time<br>*Sound of front door being opened with a key* | (Page 1) |
| *Cue 2* | **Ivor** (*off*): "Not at all, no . . ."<br>*Clink of milk bottles* | (Page 1) |
| *Cue 3* | **Caroline** finds her shoes and puts them on<br>*Phone rings* | (Page 10) |
| *Cue 4* | Music changes to party/disco type music<br>*Sound of people shouting to each other as at a party* | (Page 14) |
| *Cue 5* | Party music swells<br>*Fade party noise* | (Page 15) |
| *Cue 6* | **Douglas**: ". . . I won't have that."<br>*Shop bell sounds* | (Page 26) |

**ACT II**

| | | |
|---|---|---|
| *Cue 7* | Scene changes to the sitting-room<br>*Sound of the flat door being opened* | (Page 52) |
| *Cue 8* | The Lights fade down and come up again<br>*Phone rings* | (Page 59) |
| *Cue 9* | Start of No 26A. "Goodbye" (Reprise)<br>*Phone rings* | (Page 64) |
| *Cue 10* | **Caroline**: "Pogo, pogo, pogo."<br>*Banging from above* | (Page 66) |

MADE AND PRINTED IN GREAT BRITAIN BY
LATIMER TREND & COMPANY LTD PLYMOUTH

MADE IN ENGLAND